# White Man Walking
## An American Businessman's Spiritual Adventure in Africa

By Ward Brehm

Kirk House Publishers
Minneapolis, Minnesota

# White Man Walking
## An American Businessman's Spiritual Adventure in Africa

By Ward Brehm

Library of Congress Cataloging-in-Publication data

Brehm, Ward, 1951 -
    White man walking : an American businessman's spiritual adventure
    in Africa / by Ward Brehm.
      p. cm.
    ISBN 1-886513-47-3 (pbk.)
    1. Brehm, Ward, 1951—Journeys—Africa, Sub-Saharan. 2. Africa,
Sub-Saharan—Description and travel. 3. Brehm, Ward, 1951—Journeys-
Kenya—West Pokot District. 4. West Pokot District (Kenya)—Descrip-
tion and travel. 5. Christian biography—United States. I. Title.

BR1725.B6834A3 2003
276.762'70829'092—dc21
[B]

2003047538

Kirk House Publishers, PO Box 390759, Minneapolis, MN 55439
Manufactured in the United States of America

# Dedication

This book is dedicated
to the beautiful people of West Pokot, Kenya,
to the late Samuel Nimubona,
to my family,
and to the wider family of praying friends.

# Contents

# PART ONE

# Walking with Lodinyo

In Africa, white men don't walk. The missionaries, the doctors, the donors, when they come, they come in vehicles. They always drive. Ward was different. Ward walked. That was, to us, amazing! Ward walked with us across some of the most difficult terrain in West Pokot. No white man had ever done this before. So the message went out across the land: "A white man is walking to Mbaro." It was the first time many along the way had seen a white man. It was historic. Historic! Babies will be named after him! Ward is, to us, a legend. To this day, people are still talking about him, the white man who walked. At the end of our journey, the elders gave Ward the title *Nyakan*, meaning "a brave man who faces the unknown with only faith in God." Ward crossed not only mountain ranges, but also lines of convention. He broke barriers. He is no longer viewed as a donor. He walked, and in the process, he became one of us. Ward is our friend, our brother, a warrior, a Pokot. If his accomplishment could be reflected in his skin color, he would have come home black.

—*John Lodinyo, Pokot pastor*

# Africa

Kenya

# Introduction

*If you can't get out of it, get into it.*
*—Motto of Outward Bound*

In January of 1993, I stood with my pastor and a group of Minnesota friends on a remote hillside in Northwest Kenya across the Great Rift Valley from Uganda. I was about as far as I could be from my home, my comfort zone, and any sense of security. This was my first experience in the *real* Africa, away from Westernized cities. I was where the vast majority of Africans live their lives.

I looked at the World Vision trucks that had brought us there, and would, a few days later, bring us back to "civilization" and our way home. A thought came into my mind, and a pit formed in my stomach. "What would I do if these trucks drove away and left me here forever?" I have never experienced dread before, but I felt it that afternoon.

Eight years later, I stood on that same hillside. By my side was a tall, coal black, warrior-turned-pastor. His name was Lodinyo. Over the years, he had become my friend and, in many ways, my brother. At my back was an uninhabited Northern Kenya mountain range. Behind it were valleys and riverbeds that had never been touched by the feet of a white man.

I watched the two trucks drive away. As the dust rose behind them and they disappeared across the desert, I was "alone." I was overboard without a lifeboat. There was no way out—except as God and my African friends could lead me.

This is the story of that journey.

CHAPTER 1

# The Letter

*As iron sharpens iron, so one man sharpens another.*
*—Proverbs 27:17*

My friendship with John Lodinyo began, as friendships sometimes do, on a rocky note. Before we ever met, Lodinyo was angry with me. The root of the problem was a book I had written. *Life Through A Different Lens* was, from my point of view, an innocent personal account of the life-changing trip I took to Africa in 1993. The journey was so powerful, I felt compelled to put my experiences and impressions down on paper.

The book turned out to be a good thing for everyone—or so I thought. My church circulated it among the congregation so that members might get a better understanding of the importance of their commitment to helping communities in Africa. World Vision, an international relief and development organization, also distributed the book to prepare people for trips to developing countries. Friends, family, and even strangers who had read the book were enthusiastic and complimentary.

Then came the letter from Africa. A copy of my book had found its way into the hands of John Lodinyo, a young pastor from West Pokot, a remote area in Northwest Kenya near the Ugandan border. He had recently graduated from a Bible college and returned home to his village. Someone had given him my book, and when he read the account of my visit with his people, he became outraged (Luckily for me, we were continents apart). Though he is a man of God, Lodinyo is also a Pokot warrior, fearless and ready to confront any enemy. In his earlier life, he had left a few opponents dead on the ground. If I had known that, I wouldn't have relished the thought of being on his bad side.

The letter was clear. He thought I had a lot of nerve—visiting his village for two days, and then writing a big book as if I were an expert on his people, culture, and traditions. He objected to my use of "strong expressions" (i.e., "The Pokot are the most primitive people on earth."), and he viewed my work as a negative statement about his people. He said he was deeply hurt—and even more angry. After a few days of mulling over his comments, I realized he was right. I wrote a long, humble apology, explaining that my motive in writing the book was to make the world aware of his people, and the proud traditions and lessons I was able to gain from them, as well as the tremendous needs and struggles that are a part of their everyday life. Something in what I wrote must have made an impact on him because he accepted my apology.

Lodinyo and I met for the first time a few months later, during my second trip to East Africa. Sam Poghisio, a member of the Kenyan Parliament and a friend of mine who is also from West Pokot, had brought Lodinyo to a dinner I was attending at the Serena Hotel in Nairobi. When I first saw Lodinyo, he stood much taller than his 5-foot, 11-inch frame would indicate. He seemed carved out of an ebony tree. His posture and expression conveyed a stoic determination. This was a man not to be taken lightly. Lodinyo, it occurred to me, seemed more like a warrior than a pastor. My first impression was immediately altered when we shook hands and his face exploded into an immense smile that seemed to invite me into his very heart. We greeted each other in the traditional Pokot way—an intricate handshake followed by a full embrace. At that moment, my anxiety over what might have been a confrontation melted away.

When I spoke with Lodinyo, I once again offered my apologies for the book I had written and asked his forgiveness. My words humbled him, and he asked my forgiveness too for his harshness to me. We hugged each other, and that was the end of the conflict and the beginning of our friendship. Over the course of my subsequent annual journeys to Africa, Lodinyo and I were always able to carve out some time to be together.

## Chapter 2

# The Perplexing Invitation

*Each friend represents a world in us, a world possibly not born until they arrive, and it is only by this meeting that a new world is born.* —*Anais Nin*

L odinyo called me from Cleveland in the summer of 1999. He was in Ohio at the invitation of a group of churches. I was surprised and delighted to hear from him, and made arrangements for him to fly to Minneapolis to visit my family and me.

One of the activities I planned was an "all American" picnic. I informed Lodinyo that, in contrast to Africa, where the women do all the cooking and virtually all the work, here in America the males are in charge of barbecues, and he and I would be cooking the dinner. I could tell that he found this odd (if not downright offensive), but he indicated that he was open to any experiences we had to offer.

Our first stop was the grocery store, and I asked Lodinyo, "What would you like for dinner?" He informed me that in his culture, it is exceedingly rude to either ask for or present alternatives. He said, "You simply *give* what you have to offer, and *receive* whatever is offered." It underscored the fact that he came from a place with very few choices.

It was a perfect Minnesota summer evening. We sat together at a table on our deck, which overlooks the woods around our home. Our family held hands while Lodinyo said grace. His gentle voice resonated with the warm and appealing lilt that is common to the British English spoken by many East Africans.

In the middle of our dinner conversation, Lodinyo out of the blue asked us, "Why do you want to go to heaven?" Because of his accent, I wasn't sure I had understood what he was saying, so I asked him to repeat the question. He responded, "I want to know why you want to go to heaven." We all looked at him blankly, so he changed the question. He turned to my ten-year-old daughter, Sarah, and said, "Have you ever been hungry?" Sarah answered quite innocently, "Yes. I'm hungry right now." He looked at her more intently and asked, "Have you ever in your life been *really* hungry? Sarah responded in earnest, "I'm *really* hungry right now." Then he asked, "Have you ever worried about not having enough food?" "No," replied Sarah. Lodinyo looked at us all and quietly said, "That would be my people's definition of heaven."

He went on to say that he couldn't imagine a prettier or more peaceful setting. Everyone in the family was enjoying perfect health, and we had more food and water than we could possibly consume that day (or in a week, given the over-zealous nature of my barbecues). Coming from a background where the

*The Brehm family: Mike, Kris, Sarah, Ward, and Andy.*

word "enough" is seldom, if ever, spoken, Lodinyo recognized the tremendous blessing of not needing to worry about the next meal. He had a difficult time eating. A small tear rolled down his cheek as he talked about how guilty he felt sharing this incredible bounty, knowing that friends and family back home were having an extremely difficult time with the famine. All of us at the table were learning important lessons about real need.

My wife, Kris, then said to Lodinyo, "Well, it's wonderful that you have finally come to our home after Ward's many visits to your community." He responded, "Ward has never been to my community. And in fact, we have never been together." His comment raised the collective eyebrows of my entire family. Now I assumed Lodinyo was having some language difficulties, so I reminded him that I had been to West Pokot nine times, and five of those times I had indeed been with him. He turned his head slowly, and his eyes were piercing as he said to me, "No, we have never been together. When you come, you are always with the people you bring. You stay in a separate house on the hill. You eat with your group, sleep with your group, and only meet with us for a short time. And we know that the people in your group often laugh, talk, and smile behind our backs." I didn't know what to say. The ensuing silence confirmed the truth of his words.

Lodinyo explained that my fellow travelers and I are viewed as visitors, and when we come, the Pokot community always prepares for our arrival, scheduling meetings with the elders, and putting on the best face possible. Lodinyo was saying that, just as a Fourth of July parade is not an accurate depiction of life in America, the celebratory greetings are not a fair depiction of life in their community. While visitors are considered a blessing to the West Pokot community, and are a cause for celebration, they nonetheless are viewed as outsiders.

Lodinyo went on to challenge me to come to Africa the following year—alone. "Spend five days with me in the real bush of West Pokot. Then we will know each other, and you will know my people." He wanted me to accompany him on a hike in some of the most remote country on earth. He said, "Come and walk with me for five days, and I will take you to places that have never seen a white man or any semblance of the outside world." After such a trip, he told me, "Then we will have been together."

I looked at my family, my home, and my property—and I looked into the eyes of Lodinyo—and deep inside, my heart said, "No way."

CHAPTER 3

# A Reluctant R.S.V.P.

*True friendship is a plant of slow growth and must undergo and withstand the shocks of adversity before it is entitled to the appellation.* —*George Washington*

Lodinyo's challenge—a simple invitation—provoked in me the same inner turmoil I'd felt before my very first trip to Africa nine years earlier. I wasn't particularly concerned about the physical risks. I was more intimidated about being alone with Lodinyo and people of a completely foreign culture for that period of time. I realized, with chagrin, that this confirmed Lodinyo's earlier claim: "Ward has never been with me."

Try as I might, I simply wasn't able to shake off the challenge. It stuck in my mind like a song you can't stop humming. I fought it. I dismissed it. I tried to forget it, but it just kept coming back. My "no way" resolve was beginning to dim as I realized that this might be something I was being directed to do, even though the purpose totally escaped me. After that, the walls of resistance fell quickly. The morning I announced to my beautiful wife, Kris, that I was indeed going, she gave me a wry smile and said, "I knew you were going the moment it was suggested."

Before the trip, I made some decisions about the health and safety practices I would follow during the walk. I would carry a water purification filter designed to make any water potable. I also decided that I would fast, though I had conflicting emotions about it. On one hand, the "breaking of bread" is a critical element in East African culture. Having a meal together is symbolic of friendship and intimacy, and my not sharing in meals might be taken as an affront to those we would be encountering. On a more rational note, I thought sharing in meals would probably be dangerous for me because sanitation in the most remote areas of Africa is next to impossible. The Pokot people have developed immunity to most bacteria and organisms present in their food and water. Chances were high that I would be extremely susceptible to illness if I partook. To become sick would not only be inconvenient and burdensome to our traveling group, but downright perilous for me.

It also occurred to me that I had never experienced true hunger. The longest I had ever fasted was 30 hours during a famine relief event to raise food for the hungry. And I couldn't help but think about Lodinyo's conversation with my daughter, Sarah, about hunger. I realized this would be an opportunity to actually experience it. I would be among people for whom hunger is an everyday occurrence.

The prolonged drought in this area had resulted in famine, and the specter of starvation was descending. Perhaps by fasting for the five days, I could better identify with those whose lack of food is a central part of their lives. I also realized that fasting is Biblical: purging the body has been a source of spiritual inspiration since the beginning of time, and I had no question that fasting would add a significant dimension to the trip. As I packed my bags, I was feeling at peace with the choices I had made.

Nevertheless, as I boarded the flight, which would take me to Amsterdam and on to Nairobi, Kenya, I kept asking myself what was soon to become a familiar refrain, "What in the world am I doing?" Although I had traveled to Africa nine times before, this trip was totally different. I was going by myself. Although the flight was nearly full, mysteriously (and thankfully) no one was seated next to me. For once, I didn't need to talk to anyone; I could just be alone with my thoughts. Unfortunately, my mind was racing. I wasn't afraid, but I was unsettled. The peace had diminished, and I was feeling uncomfortable with the decision I had so resolutely made just a few months before. I was having a hard time articulating to myself just why I was going, and I was feeling at least foolish, if not reckless.

Because I had led so many group trips, being by myself seemed a luxury. I didn't have the responsibility for logistics or the countless details that need to be attended to with a group. I was responsible only for my own experiences, my own reactions, my own emotions. In Amsterdam, when I boarded the plane to Nairobi, the flight was once again full, except for an empty seat beside me. En route to Africa, my anxiety was gradually quelled and replaced by a growing sense of peace and confidence. In my thoughts, prayers, and insights, I was being silently equipped.

After having a restful evening reunion with friends, Sam and Lynn Owen, in Nairobi, I took the next afternoon flight to Eldoret, Kenya, which is about 200 miles northeast of the capitol. There I met Greg Snell, my friend since high school, just outside the security gates of the airport. We drove another hour and a half to his home in the small rural community of Kitale where his wife, Deb, was waiting for us. Greg and Deb are missionaries who left Minnesota to build up and nurture a seminary that teaches pastors in East Africa.

Once there, I began laying out and reviewing the supplies I had brought along for the trip. The spread looked like a commercial for L.L. Bean. At least one-fourth of the camping equipment I had brought for this trek was then left in Kitale for practical reasons. The lanterns, tarps, and extra clothing would be irrelevant. This was not going to be the traditional Boundary Waters Canoe Area trip! Before I left Minneapolis, a friend of mine, Brian Sullivan, provided me with one of his company's Purwater Purification Systems, which he confidently assured me would make any water potable. Western technology not withstanding, I got the notion that I might be getting in just a bit over my head. Deb remarked, "You know, Ward, I don't think the problem is the purity of water you'll be drinking, but rather the quantity. There is a severe drought in West Pokot. My guess is that you will have to carry whatever water you'll need."

Greg and Deb helped load my reduced cargo into their banged-up but road-tested four-wheel-drive Pajero. Once outside Kapenguria, the definition of "road" changed. We traversed boulder-strewn riverbeds and had to avoid huge fissures in the arid landscape. We bounced as if we were driving up and down waterfalls. Greg often turned on the windshield wipers to disperse the collected red dust that somehow managed to invade our space through any crack and cranny. During the four-and-one-half hour drive from Kitale up to West Pokot, I was engrossed in conversation with Greg about problems affecting the region, including catastrophic drought and resulting famine. Greg also questioned me regarding my own sense of calling and expectations for this journey. Expectations? I didn't have any. I again experienced a bit of anxiety. Just why was I going anyway? Was I out of my mind? Did I really believe this was a calling from God? If so, for what purpose? The questions were big and important, and the lack of answers loomed even larger.

As we traveled from Kitale, the road stretched north, a long, uneven ribbon of hard-baked clay and rock. A couple of hours into the drive, it truly became a "road less traveled," with only an occasional truck or a dilapidated bus, called a *matatu,* impossibly jammed with rural Kenyans traveling to remote and unclear destinations. As we passed the last town of any significant population worthy of placement on a map, Greg told me only two or three cars would travel this route per day. After four hours, the road had deteriorated into an endless string of gaping potholes and deeply carved ruts.

*Lodinyo*

When we finally reached the small village of Kiwawa, meaning "the place of little sheep," we were greeted by an excited and smiling John Lodinyo. Although there is no electricity or phone service,

Lodinyo knew what day I was arriving, and he was right there to welcome me. We proceeded up to Pilgrim's Place, an outpost built in the 1980s by Colonial Church in Minnesota, and made ourselves comfortable in this place that serves as a temporary shelter for the many people who visit. It's a rough but sturdy cement structure with an expansive wood deck that provides a spectacular view across the Rift Valley to Mount Kadam, the highest mountain, on the other side of the escarpment in Uganda.

Once we had finished our traditional African hugging and greeting, I proudly began laying out the fantastic array of remaining equipment from my hi-tech backpack. Lodinyo took one look at the gear I had brought along for this five-day journey, and said, "We're going to need to buy some donkeys to carry this burden!" I asked Lodinyo, "What would you normally bring on this kind of a trip?" "Nothing except my walking stick," he replied. "We make do along the way." That said, we further reduced the amount of gear to lightweight sleeping bags, one-man mosquito tents, cups for drinking, one change of clothes, insect spray, suntan lotion, power protein bars (for emergencies), and a Bible. We would also have to carry the first day's water, as there would be no wells until we reached the village of Kauriong, our destination for the night.

# Kenya

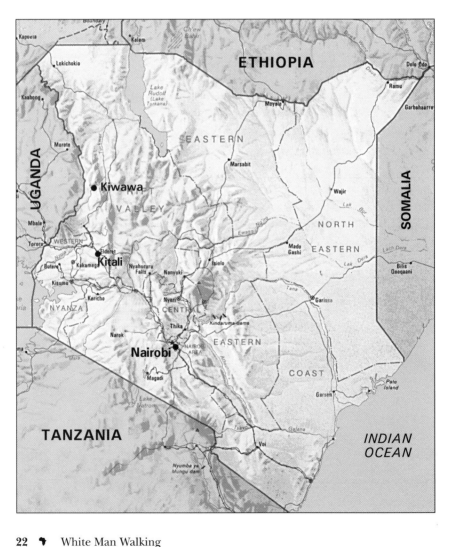

## CHAPTER 4

# Into the Vast Wide Open

*There is an astonishing contrast between the heavy perplexity that inhibits before the adventure has begun and the excitement that grips us as soon as it begins. As soon as a person makes up his or her mind to take the plunge into adventure, they are aware of a new strength they did not think they had, which rescues them from all their perplexities.*     —*Dr. Paul Tournier*

At dusk, Lodinyo went home to be with his family while Greg and I remained at Pilgrim's Place. Once again I was reminded of the divide between this "house on the hill" and the people in the village below. We slept outside on the deck, and awoke to a spectacularly clear Kenyan daybreak. I began the day with my familiar refrain, "What in the world am I doing here?" During my first and subsequent visits to West Pokot, I often had thought about what a nightmare it would be to see the World Vision vehicles pulling away and leaving me behind…alone! Now, through my own initiatives, that was precisely what was about to happen.

At dawn, we hiked down the steep hill to the village to meet up with Lodinyo. He asked whether it would be okay for one more person, Mark Lobongotum, to accompany us on the walk. I knew Mark. He had served as a sentry and armed guard during our stays at Pilgrim's Place, protecting us from the potential danger of a cattle raid from the Karamajong tribe just across the Rift Valley in Uganda. "Sure," I replied, "Mark can come. But just out of curiosity, why do we need a guard?" Lodinyo rather reluctantly replied, "Well, we really don't need a guard, but we do need a scout." "If you don't mind my asking, why do we need a scout?" I countered. Lodinyo replied, "Because where we are going, I have not been." It was then that I realized I was going off the deep end. But it was too late to change my mind. There could be no turning back.

Another friend from past visits, Michael Kimpur, the head-master at the Elementary School in Kiwawa, greeted us enthusi-astically. After reviewing the route we would be taking, he quickly summoned Mark Kasait, who heads up the clinic in Kiwawa. Mark raided the ramshackle dispensary and provided us with a plastic bag filled with rudimentary first aid items, includ-ing antibiotics, bandages, and malaria medicine. Although he had never been there himself, Mark knew of the region that we would be passing through on the other side of the mountain, and he assured us that we would unquestionably encounter medical needs in a place with no access to even basic first aid.

I also have to make a couple of small admissions here. My African friends would not allow me to leave without an emer-gency ration of energy bars. Their reasoning was simple: If I ran out of gas completely, Lodinyo would have to carry me. Also, when no one was looking, I slipped a stainless steel coffee strainer/mug and a baggie filled with Starbucks coffee in with the gear. Lodinyo had packed some traditional Chai tea, but fireside conversation—let alone my morning routine—without a steamy mug of Starbucks coffee seemed unthinkable! It didn't even cross my mind that we might not have the water to make it.

After a reluctant farewell to Greg, the three of us—Lodinyo, Mark, and I—set off on the road, walking sticks in hand and packs now heavy with water, despite our sparse provisions. The journey had begun. I was going beyond my reasonable boundaries. I was now taking an unqualified risk. I was committed—scared, excited, anxious, and even a bit proud, but definitely committed.

In some respects, West Pokot resembles a lunar landscape, bone dry. Hardy vegetation struggles to grow here. The land is beautiful in a hard, cruel way, and the dusty soil is eager to suck up any available moisture, both from the air and its inhabitants. Huge fissures and countless dried up riverbeds gash the terrain, becoming vessels for torrents of water, when and if the blessed rains fall upon these lands. The rains had not fallen for the last seven months.

Not far down the path, we encountered a group of women coming from the opposite direction. They appeared both agitated and concerned as they viewed us, pack-laden and coming from Kiwawa. The oldest woman began to point at Lodinyo and scold him in the native dialect. Both Lodinyo and Mark burst into laughter, which seemed more than a bit irreverent given the obvious concern these women were demonstrating. When I asked what the problem was, Lodinyo turned and said, "They want to know why we are torturing you!" His response didn't do much to clear up my confusion. Then he went on to say, "They're asking why we are making you carry that heavy load. What have you done wrong to deserve such a fate?" Since the temperature was nearly 100 degrees Fahrenheit, their point was well taken. I was quickly understanding the wisdom of traveling only with a walking stick.

Still early in the morning, our first stop was Lowoi, a place familiar to me. Following my very first trip to Africa, I had established a Windpump Project to support the development of sustainable water resources in the area. Lowoi was one of the communities we partnered with to construct a windpump, and I had brought businessmen here to see the site. Word of our pending arrival had spread, and small groups of children and women pocketed the outer groves of tall brush and trees. Kreswo trees are the most distinctive in this region. Growing up

to 100 feet tall in the shape of a candelabra, they look like ancient cacti on steroids. We were met by the elders of the community, who had gathered in a circle with branches in front of them. The branches would serve as a placemat for the freshly slaughtered goat that had been roasted in honor of our visit. I noticed that the goat meat seemed to have a crust or breading on it, but when the elders picked up the pieces of meat, clouds of flies dispersed and the "crust" disappeared! Flies were everywhere. To avoid any embarrassment over having to refuse food, I whispered to Lodinyo a reminder that I would be fasting during this trip. He explained to the elders my desire to experience hunger for the first time, and they nodded with both understanding and respect.

After the goat had been heartily consumed, and we had exchanged greetings, the elders presented me with a gift, a little, funny-shaped stool called a *ng'achar*. It stands just a few inches above the ground, but allows a remarkably comfortable sitting position. Although I had received many of these over the years (and they adorn shelves in my office, home, and cabin, this one would indeed come in handy over the next few days! As we thanked the elders and were about to leave, they produced yet another gift. I distinctly recall saying—arrogantly but honestly— to myself, "There is absolutely nothing these people have to offer in the way of a gift that I could possibly want. Whatever this is, I'll need to quietly chuck it along the way." My family and friends often remark how difficult it is to buy me anything. If it's something I truly want, the logic goes, I just go out and get it. While these thoughts were fresh in my mind, the elders revealed their gift: they had arranged for two men to accompany us and carry our backpacks to our destination for the evening, Kauriong, approximately six miles up the road. Although we had only traveled about four miles, I was already comprehending the high value and appropriateness of their gift!

We left Lowoi with our scout, Mark, and our backpack-carrying friends, James Limareng and Philip Limaris. As we walked, Lodinyo and I had the chance to discuss the overall situation in West Pokot, beginning with the initial relief efforts in 1984, spearheaded by Dick and Jane Hamilton, as well as Dr. Arthur Rouner and Colonial Church through World Vision. Relief is an easy concept. When people are starving to death, you feed them. Development is always much more difficult. There were many well-intentioned efforts to  provide the area with developmental necessities such as schools, clinics, and most important of all, water resources. A lot of things had been done for the people. In retrospect, more effort could have been made to involve the community with an eye towards sustainable development, with the primary focus being (as World Vision puts it today) to "build capacity." This would have allowed West Pokot to claim a greater degree of ownership and responsibility.

As the 100-degree heat became increasingly oppressive, I became more and more thankful for our "gift" of the newfound friends who seemed to be having very little difficulty carrying our load. Although I had already consumed about half of our day's water and was sweating profusely, James and Philip had yet to take even a swig, nor did they appear to be sweating at all. I am in pretty decent shape for 49. I play squash, run, and work out almost every day. But I was beginning to sense that the heat, combined with the rigors of traversing this rocky lunarscape, would be more grueling than I had anticipated. This was the first of many instances where the difference in physical acclimation was glaringly obvious to me. I was literally becoming a "fish out of water!"

The trail became narrower, with more frequent turns, as we meandered along the side of the dried up riverbed. The foliage became denser. We wound through trees, thorn bushes, and undergrowth; all were greedily competing for any precious moisture that could be extracted from the banks along the river. I looked down and noticed that both my arms were bleeding from an assortment of cuts and scrapes inflicted by the long, protruding thorns. From time to time, I thought I could see shadowed images moving through the wooded landscape. Silent and invisible, except for microsecond images out of the corner of my eye, always vanishing by the time I turned my head. It was spooky, and unsettling. More movement to my right. Again I turned sharply and saw nothing tangible. My perception was that something was moving parallel to our course. I sensed we were being watched, so I turned to Lodinyo and asked, "Do any people live nearby?" "Yes," he replied, "There are homesteads scattered throughout these hills." "Well then, why don't I see anyone?" I asked. He turned to me with a wry smile and said, "You may not see them, but they certainly can see you."

We finally reached the village of Kauriong, where we had planned to replenish our water supplies and spend the night. This would be the last of the "drilled boreholes" where fresh water is hand-pumped from 200 feet below the surface. Upon our arrival, we were informed that the aquifer beneath the borehole had been completely dry for the last five months. Lodinyo turned to me and simply stated, "I told you there was drought. This is what drought means." "So now, what do we do?" I asked, knowing that we had been counting on being able to fill our containers with enough water to last for at least the next two days. "No problem," Lodinyo replied. He gestured me to follow.

"The women have hand-dug a well in the riverbed, which has provided their water since the borehole dried up." Wearily we detoured through a maze of grass and mud homes, through parched (how could anything grow here?) and crudely sectioned garden plots, to an even smaller rocky path that led down to the river. However, there was no river. Instead, it looked like an existential painting made out of sand. Probably 40 feet wide and cut three feet down from the rocky surrounding banks was this winding ribbon of sun-bleached sand. In one of nature's cruelest hoaxes, the rainy season often deluges this geography with torrents of rain, which then tear through the land with flash flood force. As quickly as it comes, it is gone. Too much, too soon, with none remaining.

Plodding along in the ankle-deep river of sand, we made a sharp turn and saw a crudely erected "fence" of brush and bramble, which surrounded a deep, dark, five-foot diameter hole. There were flies everywhere. I couldn't believe my eyes as I

took out my small flashlight and peered down into the cavity. A makeshift ladder constructed of branches and hides reached approximately 20 feet to the bottom. The smell was unique. Not necessarily bad, although there was animal waste everywhere. The sterility of the blazing noonday sun seemed to have removed any trace of lingering odor. As I was lying on my stomach, peering down into the narrow and foreboding hole, I suddenly reflected back to my childhood when I had done something similar at a large sandbox my parents had constructed. That place also had an earthy smell, one that reminded me of earthworms and beetles. It was a stagnant odor from a part of the earth seldom explored. Sure enough, I could see the glistening of what could very loosely be defined as drinking water 30 feet below. The assorted collection of footprints and hoof prints gave further testimony to the quality of this sole source of water for the community. I turned to Lodinyo with eyes that probably didn't hide my apprehension, and he understandingly slapped me on the back. He said, "No problem, my friend. There will be freshwater springs along the riverbed tomorrow."

James approached me with a shy smile and asked if it would be possible for Philip and him to continue with us for the duration of our journey. As my eyebrows shot up, he went on to say that the packs were not a significant burden to them and that they would love to be able to complete our journey. It took me a fraction of a second to wholeheartedly welcome them as permanent additions to our traveling group.

Although we had traveled only 13 miles over relatively flat terrain, I was exhausted. Africa is big. Open spaces, long views. As the sun began to sink below the seemingly endless vista to the west of this valley, I realized that very soon Africa would not only be big, but it would also be very dark. As we sat around the glowing embers of the evening's cooking fire, the quickly approaching darkness added to the sensory collection of acrid smoke, the closeness of the animals, and the acceptance of these unlikely new friends. I found myself embraced by a tremendous sense of peace. Although I hadn't eaten anything, and the day's hike had been grueling, my spirit was mystically assured that despite the foreignness of the culture and setting I found myself in, I was somehow where I was supposed to be.

In this region of Africa, there is no twilight. Being almost directly on the equator when the sun sets, it's as if someone flips the light switch. The only source of light in this community is the sun during the day and the glow of the coals at night. There would be no moon this night. I stood up and wandered to the edge of the bramble, and gazed over miles and miles of valley floor and surrounding hills. There was only darkness.

I realized with a start that I had been here before (so to speak) on my numerous flights in and out of Nairobi en route to Amsterdam. I had passed directly over this valley a number of times, all at night. I remember the contrast between the brightly lit grids as we crossed Europe, compared to the relatively few lights visible across North Africa. From the time we reached central Sudan until we approached Nairobi, it was a continuum of blackness. I was now a part of this vast darkness. In this place, I felt I was a million miles and a thousand years away from my comfortable seat on a Boeing 747.

I returned to my carved stool, prepared a cup of evening tea, and reflected on the difficulty of the day's hike. I realized that as we traversed this seemingly forgotten riverbed, and as I found myself groping for purchase over boulders and through crevices, I was relying on my most primitive skills. In doing so, I was finding new handholds for who I was and what I was capable of. As I retied the bandana around my dust-covered forehead, I found myself at deep peace with both where I was and what I was becoming. Before moving off to the relative luxury of my sleeping bag, I took one final look at the dark faces of my traveling companions sitting around the almost dead fire. They seemed chiseled from ancient stone. While their expressions were fixed, their eyes were ever alert. These were solemn faces, determined faces, blessed faces.

Far off in the distance came the disturbing cry of some unknown beast which unsettled our community's livestock, albeit briefly. Once the snorts and jitters from my four-legged neighbors settled down, the vast darkness, silence, and that comforting sense of peace enveloped me as I drifted off into an exhausted and dreamless sleep.

# CHAPTER 5

# The Freshwater Spring

*No man with a man's heart in him, gets far on his way without some bitter, soul searching disappointment. Happy he who is brave enough to push on another stage of the journey, and rest where there are living springs of water, and three score and ten palms.*

—*Brown*

I awoke before dawn with Lodinyo lying beside me in the dark, praying aloud for the new day God was placing in our lives. He followed his prayer with a soft song in the Pokot dialect; uncharacteristically, I found myself humming along. Our plan was to leave at first light and walk until approximately noon, when the midday heat would force us to rest and find shade. We would also be exchanging the seldom-used road for a much narrower and rockier footpath. As we walked, James and Philip broke off stems from an Asiokanion tree, which proved to be flavorful and highly effective toothbrushes. I had them break off one for me, and was soon brushing along with the best of them. It wasn't Colgate, but it really did the job! These bushy-ended twigs helped explain the bright, healthy smiles characteristic of the Pokot. Lodinyo pointed out our rough route for the day to a distant mountain we would be circumventing. He told me that he had not been on the other side of the mountain, and that we would be breaking new ground together! It looked both distant and foreboding. What was I doing? As the walk became increasingly difficult, I drank more water, knowing that with every sip, our supply was shrinking. We prayed for the early arrival of the freshwater springs. I prayed particularly hard.

Four hours into our hike, James and Philip suddenly cried out and bolted from the path. Lodinyo quickly removed his bow and arrow from his shoulder, and began launching arrows into a dense, overhanging tree above our heads. It took me a while to see what he was shooting at, and then I spotted a four-foot, green Mamba snake, one of the deadliest snakes in the world. It's also known as the "ten-step Mamba," because that's approximately how many steps you have left to live after it bites! Despite obvious experience and prowess with the bow and arrow, Lodinyo missed; he followed with a barrage of rocks from the path. Feeling brave, I launched a few rocks myself, and the snake slithered higher. As it turns out, the Mamba is the only snake on earth that is known to chase humans. We abandoned this pursuit and again fell into step.

It was now 1:00 p.m. and I was parched. No moisture was evident anywhere. I was covered with a fine layer of red dust that also permeated my nose, mouth, and throat. The ground resembled rocky moonscape, and the arid soil in many places had created deep fissures and ravines. On rocks, scorpions could be seen desperately looking for shady places like crevices (or maybe pant legs), and I hoped they hadn't come to know and love sleeping bags as a potential refuge! Our path crossed and recrossed a wide, boulder-strewn, dried-up riverbed; once in a while, baboons could be seen in the trees. Although they always kept a careful distance, Lodinyo sometimes launched arrows at them. When I asked why he would want to kill a baboon, Lodinyo replied that protein is sorely missing from the local diet, so meat of any kind would be deemed a tremendous gift to the people we would be encountering ahead. He missed again, and I was secretly grateful.

As we were resting in a shady spot along the riverbed, I heard a small cry, and turned to see a young girl running from us in terror. She was wailing in the local dialect, "Help! A dead man is coming!" My companions hysterically informed me that she was referring to me! I later learned that no Caucasian had ever been in this area. I had finally found "the middle of no-where!" Though a few of the Pokot elders had been to Kiwawa and seen Caucasians, the women and children were glimpsing a white person for the first time. The little girl stopped about 100 yards away, and despite her younger brother's willingness and courage to come over to us and curiously touch me, she would have nothing to do with me. In her mind, I was a very strange alien creature. This would be the first of many "first encounters" with people who were both surprised and clearly shaken by the sight of white skin. I was experiencing what it's like to be a minority. Despite the fact that the sun was quickly tanning my white skin, I was still far from being ebony. From here on, I would be a carnival attraction to a people whose scenery and experiences rarely, if ever, change. Everything in this land is constant, with the exception of the very occasional rain that is cruelly and quickly sucked back into the ground.

We walked on. At a turn in the riverbed, I saw before us a pool of opaque, muddy water that appeared to be a mirage in an otherwise totally arid environment. But without so much as a pause, my African friends quickly disrobed and ran splashing into the tepid water. Being parched both on the inside and out, I quickly joined them and took delight in the "bath," despite the many surrounding footprints and droppings from goats, hyenas, baboons, camels, and cattle. I looked back into the murky water with a sudden horror. I remembered the warnings against swimming in Afri-can lakes due to the many water-borne parasites and diseases. My  mind was filled with thoughts of cholera, typhoid fever, and an endless parade of unnamed maladies. Maybe this was why I had been given all those immunizations before I came. Would they work? My mind continued to race, and new visions of that horribly insidious African parasitic disease came into focus. Six months from now, would some foot-long parasite be gnawing its way out of my armpit? What was I doing here?

As we were drying off in the blazing afternoon sun, I said that I hoped we would find drinking water soon—and was unceremoniously told that this was the "freshwater spring" they had promised! "You mean we all just took a bath in our water supply?" I asked incredulously. My thoughts immediately turned to my friend, Brian, and the water filter he had insisted I bring along. The directions on the purifier warned that if you suspected that you might be within 50 yards of animal droppings, you should filter the water twice. In this pool, there were floating clumps, and dung was floating all along the water's edge. I knew this murky liquid would need a miraculous transformation if I were to be able to consume it and live to tell the tale. I offered one of my many silent prayers as we began pumping water through the filter, and it was immediately answered as crystal clear water poured out the other end of the pump! I have never been so relieved.

While we were restocking our water supply, an elder from the area came across our party and stopped to talk. Throughout the trip, I viewed it as a tremendous compliment that at least 90 percent of the conversation was in the Pokot dialect, and thus I never felt that I was a "guest," but rather just part of the group, despite my inability to understand most of what was being said. Whenever I asked, an explanation was promptly given, but never volunteered. This allowed me to spend an enormous amount of time with the people, yet to be within my own thoughts.

One Pokot refrain that became very familiar to all of us was, *Kai kai tasa tagh,* which means, "Press On." It came in very handy following the periodic rest stops along the way. In fact, *Kai kai!* became the requisite salute following each much-revered rest stop.

I was convinced that the bath had left me dirtier than I was before I took it. As we were drying off, a tall Pokot man about 30 years old approached our group. He was startled when he saw me, but was determined not to show fear. This elder (yes, you are an elder at 30 when your life expectancy is 41) informed us that he was on his way to Alale, the site of the airstrip that past windpump teams have used, located about 15 miles away. He said that the drought had now resulted in famine, and he was going there to determine whether the rumors of relief food being distributed were true. His name was Domongoria. He said he had been outside this canyon many times bartering for animals and communicating with surrounding groups of people, so he had seen a white man every now and then. He said that the vast majority of those we would be encountering along the way had not. He seemed to take a certain amount of pleasure in the fact that there would be some consternation among his family and friends as we traveled together. Domongoria said he could accompany us back up the canyon, and he invited us to stay with his family.

In this area (as throughout much of the world), visitors are viewed as a tremendous blessing. Lodinyo explained that people

here sometimes pray, "God, bring us visitors," because they know they cannot make it in the world alone. They believe that the feat of entertaining visitors will bring blessings, and they want those blessings. "May your animals prosper. May they give birth to twins!" That's what they want: stability, security, peace, and a good future for their children—identical to the hopes and dreams of all human beings. Everybody wants to be blessed.

All visitors from within or outside the community are treated with utmost kindness and hospitality. The Pokot believe that to do otherwise would anger the gods who are the source of their cattle, goats, sheep, women, and children. A Pokot therefore does everything possible to make visitors feel at home away from home. This hospitality typically is demonstrated in smiles, songs, and the slaughter of their finest animals.

The heat was becoming increasingly oppressive, and we found ourselves stopping about every 45 minutes to rest, parking ourselves on our carved stools under the occasional shade tree. I later learned that these "breaks" were entirely for my benefit. Typically, a Pokot can travel all day without stopping even once! During one of our respites, a young warrior (approximately 16 years old) came down the path and spotted me. Although it is customary for warriors to show no fear, this one was visibly shaken. My traveling companions burst into laughter when he exclaimed in Pokot, "Wow! He looks almost like a real human being." I learned quickly that these people were reluctant to look directly at me. They would rather take sidelong glances when they thought I wasn't looking. I later learned that, in the Pokot culture, to look someone directly in the eyes— especially a visitor or one of social rank or age—is a sign of disrespect and incivility. However, this didn't stop them from making observations. Sometimes when I would get up and move from a sitting position on a rock, they would exclaim in amazement, "He walks, too!" Although these encounters would continue to be a novelty, they gave me an unforgettable moral lesson on how isolated it feels to be a minority and discriminated against (innocently and non-intentionally). I was different in every way—looks, language, color—different in every way except the smile.

We came upon another "freshwater spring." It seemed even murkier and smellier than the reservoir where, with the help of modern science, I had turned "water into wine." James reloaded his three-gallon container (which he was lugging, along with my pack, with seeming ease) from this blackish hole. Without using any filter, he proceeded to drink what appeared to be his only water of the day. As I waited for him to writhe in agony and die, he informed me that these were the only water sources available for more than ten miles. It was obvious that he and the Pokot people had no apparent biological problems due to the pot-pourri of microscopic critters and bacteria lurking within each cupful. I harbored no such confidence in my own Western digestive system, but I realized that if the filter failed, there would be no alternative. It wasn't a pleasant thought.

We stopped at a huge Ongo'owin tree with branches that extended out more than 20 feet. Lodinyo said we should rest there until the sun had gone over the ridge before going on to Domongoria's homestead in the village of Chemoikut. It turned out Domongoria lived approximately two miles in the opposite direction from which we were traveling, but I was the only one who seemed to notice as we detoured through even rockier terrain. We finally came upon approximately two acres of flat ground surrounded by a *kasar*, an effective hedge constructed of

bramble, wicket, thorn, and Katoo branches. When the gate is closed at night, it keeps the inhabitants (including people, camels, goats, and cows) safe from surrounding predators.

Domongoria introduced me to his family, which included three wives and 12 children. Each wife cooked, and maintained her individual *kopocheptupon*, which is a home assembled with grass, mud, and manure. The Pokot are largely nomadic, meaning that all of their dwellings are temporary and typically abandoned after two to six months when the cattle seek more fertile places to graze. As a result, we would come across many uninhabited Pokot "ghost towns."

That evening Domongoria told us that in honor of our visit he would be killing a goat. It isn't until you realize how very little the people have that you can appreciate the magnificence of such a gift. Because I was fasting, I wasn't able to partake in the feast. Again the explanation was given and graciously accepted. Nevertheless I learned a thing or two about the diet of the Pokot people.

There are little (if any) agricultural opportunities due to the barrenness of the land, although figs can be gathered during rainy season along the riverbed. Sometimes bees provide honey, or the infrequent baboon is brought down with an arrow or a rock. One staple, when available, is the termite. Following the first long rains, the huge winged ants come up from their nests buried deep within the ground. The nests are usually adjacent to huge and towering anthills called *tulwos*, which are formed from the excrement and saliva of the ants and the red dust from the ground. These hills can be as tall as ten feet. During a drought, the Pokot women will pound on the ground to imitate the sound of falling rain; sometimes they are successful in their attempts to fool the ants to the surface. The women fashion ingenuous "traps" by lining the escape routes with the smooth, extremely sticky leaves of the Iwak plant; the leaves cause the ants to stick or fall back so they can easily be collected. The ants are then dried and kept as a food reserve for a time when the rains stop.

Nearly 100 percent of the food consumed by the Pokot is in the form of blood or milk. Domongoria's family subsists on approximately three gallons of blood each day. During "good times," the blood is mixed with milk from the animals, but due to the drought and resulting lack of any vegetation, the animals had stopped producing milk, thus reducing the people's diet to only the blood of the animals. To get the blood, a small incision is made in the neck of the chosen "donor," and the daily requirement is collected in a crude pot. The pot of blood is either set aside in the sun or briefly cooked, which coagulates the blood into a consistency that can be scooped and consumed by hand. I had always been aware of the importance of animals to the Pokot in that they represented the only true measure of wealth, but only now did it finally make sense. These animals provide life itself. When they die, the food chain ends. It's over. The lights go out in the supermarket.

Domongoria invited me to the ritualistic killing of the goat, which proved to be an adventure in itself. Lodinyo carefully cut the artery in order to conserve the precious blood for later consumption. While the animal was still kicking, our host lowered his mouth to the animal's neck and drank directly from the source! It wasn't your everyday Sunday brunch!

After the blood was drained, the goat was carefully slaughtered with the precision of a Mayo Clinic surgeon. Lodinyo informed me that almost every part of the goat would be used and consumed, as is also true of sheep, cows, and camels. Lodinyo said the parts that cannot be eaten include the hard covers of the hooves, which are removed so that the meat underneath can be consumed. Also, the bones and eyeballs cannot be used, but the bone marrow and the meat around the eyeballs can.

I politely retired to the tent sites, which were located near the pens shared by two rambunctious camels and a number of suspicious goats. I was hungry, but in a new and different way. I could tell that my system needed food, but I had no appetite— no doubt due to the menu selection. It had now been more than two days since I had eaten, and it seemed that while my body craved food, my mind and soul were expanding with startling clarity and vision. I felt physically weak, but spiritually strong.

After dinner, I rejoined the group. We sat around a small, but nevertheless welcoming campfire made up of a tiny pile of glowing coals. Unlike the roaring bonfires of home, even firewood is used very sparingly. Like everything else in Africa, no more is expended than absolutely necessary. Again most of the evening conversation was in the Pokot language, which allowed me the opportunity to collect my thoughts and process my various experiences. As I wrote in my journal, I was increasingly aware that the environment I had entered was considerably more alien and discomforting than I had ever imagined, and fraught with very real risk. The refrain, "What am I doing here?" returned to my thoughts.

Later that evening, as we lay on top of our sleeping bags (the earth seemed to radiate heat, even at night), Lodinyo told me about himself. Lodinyo's father was killed during a Pokot/Karamajong cattle raid. His mother, two brothers, and two sisters were extremely poor, living in Uganda when the early 1980s famine began. The entire community was profoundly affected. Eventually their animals died, and towards the end, their stay in Uganda reduced them to scavenging for anything edible and eating rats. They were finally forced to eat wild Loma berries that are extremely toxic. They are so poisonous that unless they are boiled for 12 hours or longer, they kill. Nevertheless, prior to what was known to be an agonizingly long and difficult journey, the clan gorged themselves to the point of fooling their bodies into a false sense of nourishment and strength. They had received word that relief food distributions were taking place in Kiwawa, Kenya, and the entire community began the six-day walk across the scorching and barren northern Great Rift Valley.

Lodinyo does not know his date of birth, but recalls that when he was about ten years old, the entire community of Loro, Uganda, which numbered about 1,000, migrated together. They would rise at 3:00 or 4:00 a.m. and begin walking to avoid the devastating heat of the East African sun. They would stop before noon in the relative shade of dried up riverbeds that crisscross the terrain. They had nothing to eat. They would chew on old animal skins that would activate the salivary glands and trick their bodies into feeling nourished. They foraged what little water they could find in hand-dug wells in the arid riverbeds. There were many deaths. Most people died at night; they simply didn't wake up. There were no funerals or burials. It was a time for the living. There was a desperate struggle for survival. Nearing collapse after six days, the survivors stumbled and nearly fell into the emergency feeding camps established by World Vision.

The famine and the feeding continued for two years. It was during this time that Lodinyo went to his first school, which had also been started by World Vision. His family returned to Uganda, but Lodinyo, who was very bright and wanted an education, asked to stay. He became a Christian and was baptized in 1982. As he would recall, it meant very little to him. At the time, he really didn't have an understanding of the significance of the event; he was baptized because it was part of his tradition. I realized this is often true in our culture as well. The missionaries were deported in 1988, and Lodinyo returned to Uganda and became a renowned warrior. He was well known for his bravery, and he killed many enemies. He was frequently shot at, but never hit.

The seemingly ageless conflict between the Pokot and the Karamajong had escalated from bows and arrows to spears, and then to AK-47s. Huge caches of arms had been left behind following Idi Amin's reign of terror in Uganda, which ended in the 1980s, and these caches had fallen into the hands of various tribesmen. During one historic battle in 1988, Lodinyo found himself in a perilous situation. He, his brother, and about 20 other Pokot warriors walked into an ambush. They were surrounded and greatly outnumbered by Karamajong adversaries. There was no way out. He and his brother would most certainly die here in enemy territory. In those terrifying circumstances, Lodinyo came to know God in a personal way. In the midst of the turmoil, Lodinyo gave himself to God, and prayed that if God would rescue him from this doom, he would devote the rest of his life to Him (This sounded like a prayer I'd said at various crises in my own life). In any event, Lodinyo, his brother, and all the others miraculously escaped.

Good to his word, Lodinyo became a true and committed follower of Jesus. He attended four years of Bible College in Mombassa, on the southern coast of Kenya. His "deal" with God was consummated as he studied the Bible and grew in his faith.

After college, he was tempted to accept a pastoral position in Mombassa, which would have been a much more hospitable location to bring up his children. He could have lived in a modern house with running water and electricity and all that goes with it, including a refrigerator and television. Despite the temptation to choose a secure and comfortable location for himself and his family, Lodinyo felt a strong sense of calling to his own people, the Pokot, many of whom had never heard the name of Jesus. So he and his wife and children returned to Kiwawa.

As it often mysteriously happens, one of the day's Bible verses that Lodinyo and I read together spoke directly to his heart, and has subsequently become the verse that guides his life:

> You look to the left (Mombassa); you look to the right (Nairobi). But a voice behind you is directing you. "This is the way (West Pokot). Walk in it!" —Isaiah 30:21

I heard Africa that night as a living and breathing creature. The nearby camels and goats were tethered, but restless, as the moonless midnight, a backdrop to a billion stars, grew near. I felt like I was in the belly of a huge slumbering giant with the pitch-black canopy above. Only the last dying coals from the campfire gave the semblance of any light whatsoever. The air was void of any remnant of moisture, causing me to envision the vast deserts of Africa to the north.

I heard a high-pitched scream of an unknown animal. It ended so quickly that its memory lasted far longer than it had in reality; it was the cry of some unknown beast in the death throes of an equally unknown vanquisher. The night seemed to live and breathe in an alluring and seductive way replete with implied danger that echoed the mysteries of centuries past. It was instructive in the unforgiving nature of a land untouched by the soft hand of civilization. It was ageless, yet so present. And it was wonderfully big.

# Chapter 6

# My Day as a Cat

*Less is more. —Robert Browning*

*Never allow the thought, "I am of no use where I am," because you certainly can be of no use where you are not. —Oswald Chambers*

Instead of waking up from a dream, I felt as if I was waking up to a continuing one in this far away place. The sun broke dramatically over the hills, illuminating the picturesque landscape with a thousand shades of brown. The seemingly innocent clear blue sky gave veiled warnings of the brutal heat to come, but right then I welcomed the relative cool dawn air and the fresh promise of a new day.

The ever-smiling and thoughtful James presented me with a pot of boiling water for morning coffee. As I looked suspiciously towards the muddy pot on the coals, he assured me the water was from my filtered reservoir. I took delight in the familiar comfort of this morning "coffee" ritual, which now included a bit of freshly drawn camel's milk. Starbucks could learn a lesson from this exotic "Pokot latte." While I was sitting on my now greatly appreciated hand-carved stool, Lodinyo looked at me with his wide eyes and beaming smile and said, "I am sorry to inform you, Ward, but, as it pertains to our route for this journey, I seem to have made a gross miscalculation!" After discussing the planned itinerary with Domongoria, Lodinyo had discovered that reaching our next planned destination, Kasei, would necessitate a "killer walk." When I responded that I felt really good and strong and up to the challenge, Lodinyo replied, "You don't understand, my friend. If we take this walk, it will kill us dead!"

I quickly adjusted my thoughts to his way of thinking. Lodinyo said he had learned that there would be no access to any water for the duration of the next two-day hike to our ultimate destination of Mbaro. The original route would have taken us at least three days. There was no way we could travel that long or far without additional water. He said that the advisable alternative would be to remain in this place. We would need to spend the entire next day drinking as much water as possible and resting in an attempt to "get strong" for what promised to be an arduous, dry, and exhausting trek to our ultimate destination. I told him the obvious, that any input from me would be totally uninformed. I said I would accept and trust all remaining decisions that came from him and his friends.

It was an interesting day in that we did absolutely nothing. I would liken it to the average day spent by my cat. I have often wondered how any creature could live so aimlessly. A cat gets up in the morning, wanders around, and makes an occasional stop at the food and water dish. Lots of naps, lots of stretching, a bit of poking around, and not much else. At about 9:00 a.m. the sun broke from the surrounding hills on Domongoria's settlement, and the resulting immediate increase in temperature gave promise to another 100-degree scorcher. We decided to wander back to the Ongo'owin tree along the riverbed for shade. A sense of anxiety started creeping up on me as I realized that this would be a day filled with nothing but "rest." I'm unaccustomed to much, if any, idle time in my life back home. I don't rest much, and I wasn't too sure I was going to enjoy a whole day of "down time." As we were walking down Domongoria's path in the riverbed, James told me that he had some questions. I asked what they were, and he shook his head and somewhat timidly said he wasn't ready to ask them yet. I realized that we had plenty of time.

The Pokots took nothing but their walking sticks, while I packed up a few things, including sunglasses, my camera, a water bottle, and my Dopp kit for the promised visit to the "swimming hole." I also brought along my Bible, a list of Scripture verses that had been prepared for me by friends for the trip, and a book I was reading which recounted the genocide in Rwanda, the country I would be visiting in just a week. We settled in under the tree, and throughout the day I learned about the people and the culture of West Pokot.

I'm not sure where in the timeline of the development of world civilization this place and lifestyle would fit. It certainly pre-dates the birth of Christ by a substantial margin. In fact, anthropologists have discovered some of the earliest evidences of mankind here. The people are nomadic, and live a life of day-to-day survival based on intuition and ingenuity. There are few (if any) vestiges of wealth in this culture, other than cattle, goats, and camels. The truly poor are those who die from lack of food and medicine. We would later encounter this level of poverty.

When severe drought comes to West Pokot, the extremely difficult living environment quickly becomes lethal. The Pokot are pastoralists and their animals represent the only buffer between starvation and life. The people have learned to "diver-

sify their portfolios" to survive. Cows are most revered because they quickly breed and produce large quantities of milk. In a drought, however, they are the first animals to perish. Goats are the second most important commodity because, although they are scrawny and stingy with both blood and milk, they are much hardier in severe conditions. Camels are by far the most durable, but they breed much more slowly. In times of drought and the inevitable famine which follows, these animals are walking "pantries," supplying blood, milk, urine (for sterilization), and meat when they eventually die.

Life in the remote areas of Africa is harsh. It's a constant battle with nature, and the thin line between life and death leaves very little room for individualism. The community must and does come first. Always. This sense of community is apparent in all aspects of Pokot life. Although families live considerable distances from one another, to the extent that any family's problems are known, they immediately become the problems of the entire community. What little resources they have are shared in times of need. The concept of a nursing home or an orphanage would be incomprehensible to them. The older a man is, the more revered he is for his wisdom and experience. Unfortunately, at this time, the same is not true for women; they are regarded as "property." Children are the responsibility of not only the parents, but also the collective society. The ways and customs are based on lessons and wisdom that are paramount to survival itself. Reputation is everything. These are very strong people living in an extremely difficult environment.

I was able to discuss the traditional belief system, with Lodinyo working as a translator for Domongoria. The Pokot people believe that when you die, your spirit leaves your body and inhabits a place near and above Mount Kadam, the highest peak within eyesight in that region. Beyond that, it's not clear what the afterlife entails other than you no longer have a body.

Seeing these people who have never heard the name of Jesus or been exposed in any way to the Gospels, I was reminded of Eugene Peterson's New Testament translation from Romans 2:14-16.

*If you sin without knowing what you're doing, God takes that into account.*

*When outsiders who have never heard of God's law, follow it more or less by instinct, they confirm its truth by obedience. They show that God's law is not something alien, imposed on us from without, but woven into the very fabric of our creation. There is something deep within them that echoes God's yes and no, right and wrong. Their response to God's yes and no will become public knowledge on the day God makes his final decision about every man and woman. The message from God that I proclaim through Jesus Christ takes into account all these differences.*

We would have the opportunity later that evening to actually test out this theory.

James, finally comfortable, got around to asking me questions. The first one was, "Are there any poor people in America?" That stopped me. I replied that I needed a little time before I could answer. He smiled. After considering it for a while, I said there were poor people in my country, but the poverty was on a different scale and not limited to physical adversity, but also included moral and emotional poverty. I tried to explain moral poverty in terms of pride, immorality, greed, and materialism. I could tell that these notions were difficult for him to comprehend. For him, poverty is not having enough resources to survive. He constantly referred to the notion of people "struggling." For all people in the remote areas of West Pokot, life is a fight for survival.

He then went on to ask how a poor person in America could improve his situation. I explained that an extremely strong work ethic, physical strength, and a fierce commitment to bettering one's circumstances are character traits that might make a person successful.

James was confused when I spoke of racism and bigotry in America. "Do they steal each other's cows? Is segregation like when white missionaries come and they live in a separate place?" I pondered and replied, "Not exactly."

Despite the lack of any type of formal education as we know it, the Pokot are among the most capable people I have ever encountered. They stay alive because of tremendous ingenuity, basic survival instincts, common sense, and calculated risk-taking. Their children learn through active experiences. They are taught life skills—how to find water and food, accurately throw a spear and shoot an arrow, and erect a temporary shelter. They benefit from a culture that is exceedingly rich in social interaction and fiercely loyal in extended family support. If I were to be dropped into their environment, fully alone and without assistance and guidance, I wouldn't survive. I'm sure of it. I'm equally sure that they would survive—and maybe even thrive—in our environment, because of their personal character attributes.

We took a short excursion towards a spring, and I noticed a simple log structure in the arm of a tree. It was a crafted bee-hive, with the prize being honey. Every possible source of nourishment available is both known and carefully revered. Pokot people don't merely appreciate their environment; they are totally dependent upon it and one with it. There is a timeless rhythm pulsating through this canyon that dates back to the beginning of humanity. It is a land currently disrupted by pro-longed and severe drought. The normally difficult lives of its inhabitants are now pushed to the very edge of survival itself. There are no reserves. No savings accounts. No Social Security. What there is today is a fierce determination to survive as a community. It occurred to me that my footsteps should be extremely light as I passed through this valley so unaffected by the outside world.

We went to restock my water supply, and to my horror the filter failed! The directions said it would last from three to six months, but that promise clearly wasn't intended to include the sludge we were attempting to transform. The filter was almost totally plugged, and only an occasional drop of water was pass-ing through. At the last minute, my friend Brian had added another filter to my pack, "just in case," and I'm confident that his gesture may have saved my life.

We tried again. This time we wrapped my bandana around the intake valve for added filtration and first put the water into the three-gallon jug and allowed it to sit for a couple hours so that at least some of the sediment could settle. It worked! I was more than a little relieved. Now I needed this filter to hold out for at least three more days.

We went for our afternoon swim in the multi-purpose mud hole, and although I soaped and shampooed, I again doubted that I had emerged any cleaner than before I went in. I was nevertheless refreshed. The wives of Domongoria brought down remnants of the last evening's goat feast. My friends immediately consumed the food. I was ordered by Lodinyo to eat one of the protein bars I had brought along at his insistence. He told me from the onset that fasting during a walk like ours could be dangerous, and if I were to collapse, it would be his responsibility to carry me out! He said that as part of our getting "strong" for the next day's journey we had to feed our bodies. I actually felt a physical surge as the protein hit my system.

We talked and napped, and in between, Lodinyo would pull out his Bible and read Scripture to us. James, who has no opportunity for employment (because there are no employers), has a dream of opening a medical dispensary in the region. He has worked as an unpaid helper for the Kiwawa Clinic and developed an effective, if rudimentary, understanding of the most common local ailments and associated remedies. I began referring to him as "Dr. James." Whenever he encountered medical problems (which were many), he would observe and consult with the patient before prescribing very basic medications (ibuprofen, antibiotics, malaria medicine, and bandages), which had been prophetically given to us prior to the journey.

In the United States, we debate the merits of national health insurance. In this area, there is no health care whatsoever. No emergency rooms, no drugs, no aspirin, no bandages, nothing. And health problems here are overwhelming. Lodinyo told me that back in the relative civilization of Kiwawa, his four-wheel-drive vehicle serves as the only available "ambulance" in the region. He is often awakened in the middle of the night by people bringing the casualties of accidents and disease to him for transport to Kapenguria. Frequently, young men are brought to him with severe wounds inflicted during the raiding attacks among the Pokot, Karamajong, Turkana, and Sabiny tribes that vie for pasture land and water in this quadrant of Northwest Kenya along the Uganda border. Many times they arrive too late.

And here, where the road ends and the winding footpath at the entrance of this valley behind the large mountain begins, all motorized access ends as well. Previously, when his only vehicle was a motorcycle, Lodinyo and another pastor would "sandwich" the patient between them for the torturously bumpy ride to the clinic.

The average Pokot wife gives birth to ten children. Six of the ten die in childbirth or before the age of two. Only two of the ten reach adulthood. Obviously, there is no access to anything approaching sterile conditions. Simple traumatic injuries cause permanent crippling, infections, or even death. Malaria, virtually unknown to the developed world, is the number one killer here. Other killers are the usual suspects: cholera, tuberculosis, polio, diarrhea, and common infections. While preventative measures as well as treatments exist, they are only heard about, and unavailable in a region accessible only by footpaths. Just one more example of the razor's edge between life and death.

Convenience, let alone luxury, is a foreign notion. Obviously, there are no phone lines or electricity in the bush, although the cell phone culture may not be that far away. Communication is still through face-to-face encounters, and the network is fast and efficient. Virtually every village we passed through had advance notice of our coming. We didn't see many people along the way, but we were definitely seen. The message went all over: "A white man is walking!" The villagers could not imagine it, because the white men they had heard about never walked. They always drove.

As we continued our journey, small things became apparent. There is no refrigeration. Ice is unknown. I recalled that when Lodinyo was at our home, he always requested no ice in his water glass because the coldness hurt his teeth. Pictures from my wallet of my family skiing in Colorado were viewed with amazement. The Pokot are not able to preserve anything. There is no salt. The people smell like people, because there is no soap, let alone cosmetics or perfume.

There is also no violent crime. As we were later to learn, there is theft, but stealing is punishable by death, or perhaps worse, banishment. There are no drugs, no alcohol, no AIDS, or sexually transmitted diseases. Adultery is also punishable by death. The only vice I could discern was the tradition of cattle raiding. The Pokot and their enemies—the Karamajong, Turkana, and Sabiny tribes—are both perpetrators and victims in a rivalry over the livestock in the region. Historically, these tribes have *each* believed that *all* the cows are their exclusive gift from God. Therefore, the cattle raids and associated killings are not thought of as crimes, but rather as heroic attempts to repossess what they feel is rightfully theirs.

The Pokot culture is polygamous, but it was not always that way. Originally each man had one wife. But over time women began to outnumber men, leading up to the current five-to-one ratio. For unknown reasons, male babies have a much higher mortality rate, and additionally over the past several hundred years, many male warriors have been killed in the numerous, often-deadly cattle raids on neighboring tribes. In recent years the mortality rate in these ongoing battles has increased significantly with the escalation from spears to automatic weapons.

The typical "bride price" dowry is between 15 and 30 cows, depending on the beauty and strength of the young woman, as well as the family's reputation for wisdom and hard work. Coming up with enough cows for the initial bride price is problematic and has been an unfortunate incentive for cattle raiding. Usually the father and older brothers are willing to help with the "down payment" of a few cows, but each man is on his own for second and subsequent wives.

Although difficult to understand from our society's viewpoint, the first wife always celebrates the taking of additional wives. She always retains her Number One status as head of the family, and then can delegate the more difficult and onerous jobs to the younger and stronger additions to the family. Each wife builds and maintains her individual home, which also houses her direct offspring, though the upbringing of the children is a shared responsibility of the entire family.

It is not uncommon for marriage to occur shortly following puberty, as the average life expectancy for a Pokot is around 40 years. We encountered numerous piles of rocks alongside the footpaths, which were graves. Domongoria explained that all elders are buried, whereas women and children who die are typically left in the wilderness as part of the continued cycle of nature.

Lodinyo told me that the Pokot people have always had only one supreme God who is everywhere. Traditionally, they have offered burnt sacrifices at the foot of the "Holy Mountain," Mount Kadam. They also have had great historic prophets. Listening to Lodinyo, I realized with a start that the Pokot lifestyle closely resembles that of the Old Testament. When some of these legends were related to me, I was struck by how many of their oldest recollections seem to mirror Deuteronomy. One in particular involved an ancient leader named Lomorsai who is renowned for leading the Pokot people to their present location during a time of tremendous famine and hardship. Along the way, they needed to cross a huge and raging river. Lomorsai was able to stop the river temporarily and allow safe passage of the people. How often our heritages intersect, I thought.

This whole land has an ancient sacredness about it. In October 2000, the renowned anthropologist, Richard Leakey, and his team discovered what might be the oldest human skull to date on the shores of nearby Lake Turkana. It seems appropriate that this place might indeed be the "cradle of mankind."

As we sat with our expanding group of friends, I suddenly noticed a Boeing 747 jetliner over our heads, in the flyway, probably at 45,000 feet. "So what do they think that is?" I asked Lodinyo. Turning to me with a smile on his face, he said, "I don't know, I'll ask." The Pokots talked among themselves and then responded. Lodinyo translated, "They don't know." I wasn't about to let them off the hook and said, "I want to know what they think each day when they see these planes flying high in the sky over their heads." After being posed the question via Lodinyo, the elders took a bit more time in their discussion. Their reply got a big laugh out of Lodinyo, as he turned and said, "They don't care." What a great answer! I laughed, too, as I pondered the wisdom in their response.

In the middle of the afternoon, some heavy clouds rolled over the surrounding mountains, which at the moment looked a lot like the spine of a partially buried, prehistoric dragon. There were a few sharp peaks, but mostly humped and rounded summits that resembled the shoulders of a slumbering beast. Shadows from the billowing clouds painted pockets in the valley with new and darker shades of beige and brown. Suddenly, it began to rain. Our small party, which had grown to eight people, was ecstatic. They sang, they danced, they literally jumped with joy. I felt mildly inconvenienced, as I always do when caught in a rain shower, but I almost immediately changed my perspective. This was the first moisture to touch the ground since the previous August, nearly seven months earlier. This was more than a refreshing shower. It was a gift from the heavens that would save lives.

A woman coming towards us across the riverbank 100 yards out caught sight of me, and after much laughter and incessant coaxing on our part, she was finally convinced to come and join our group. We were positioned underneath a large rock over-

hang, out of the rain. It wasn't until a few moments after she joined us that I noticed a tiny baby wrapped in the traditional *anapet*, fashioned out of goat hide, around her shoulders. She kept repeating the word, *Ilat*, which I did not understand. The group was laughing almost hysterically and finally explained to me that she thought that I was *Ilat*, their god of rain. She was convinced that I had come from Uganda, bringing blessed rains with me. I immediately insisted that they set the record straight and explain that I was merely a friend of theirs from a distant place, who was walking with them. I'm not sure she bought it. Nevertheless she seemed to relax as we watched the blessed rain fall upon the parched earth.

The woman, whose name was Cheptilak, then explained that she lived in a remote ravine about three miles away and that she had come for the daily water for her family from the "well-used spring." It seemed like a long distance to walk each day, until Lodinyo advised me that many of the women travel more than ten miles at least every other day because all other water resources have dried up. While we struggle with the issue of equality and women's rights in America, the plight of African females, whose functions are deeply embedded within traditions, seems to me particularly unjust. Nevertheless, I feel an obligation to be "hands off" when it comes to addressing cultural differences. It is dangerous to tinker with cultural practices because there is a high probability that any changes to these practices will have a negative impact and exponential effect on the socioeconomics and culture. Africa is full of tough issues with no easy answers.

I noticed that Cheptilak wore a beaded necklace, as did most of the women we encountered. Where did it come from, I wondered. As it turned out, even this most remote region isn't immune from commerce. On occasion, traders from Kitale pass through, bartering cloth and beads for goats. From the cloth, women make their colorful dresses called *leso*. This also helped explain the sandals called *kwegh* that seem ever present in East Africa. They are ingenuously engineered from car tires, cost about 60 cents, and last an average of seven years. That's a lot of mileage from a little tread!

Cheptilak went on to tell us that her family was struggling. Many of their animals had died as the result of the prolonged drought, and her husband had bartered the remaining few for food. Without livestock to bleed for food, their savings account was empty. They had no reserves. Her husband was off looking for food. They were at the end of a very tenuous rope. Because they live in such a remote location, Domongoria and the others in the community had not known of their plight. We promised we would visit them on our way out of the canyon the following morning. Her eyes expressed relief. She indicated that her children were "too thin." That was an understatement.

We returned to Domongoria's homestead in time to see the sun framing the mountains. The outlines of the huge, flat-

topped Sess trees that served as tall sentinels to his clearing, formed spidery shadows in the dying afternoon sun. I was actually starting to feel at home here with my new friends. I realized that although I hadn't tackled a long "to do" list, and in fact hadn't done anything at all, I had indeed had a wonderful day, rich with insight and fellowship with Lodinyo and the others.

Unbelievable even to Lodinyo, Domongoria decided to sacrifice another goat in celebration of the visitors. I now realized and appreciated the extravagance of the act, as well as the importance of the notion of being blessed by visitors. The sense of gratitude was very real here. While the goat was butchered, cooked, and devoured in short order, I retired to a rocky overlook to write, read, and reflect. Although my thoughts were jagged and non-symmetrical, they somehow all fit together. I was at peace. The unanswered questions were much less important than the notion of being in the right place at the right time despite not knowing why. It was both indefinable and yet very real at the same time. Again, I took it as a high compliment that the majority of the conversation during the day had been in the Pokot dialect, and that I was accepted as part of the team, albeit a strange part.

I had been saving my biggest question for the moment following dinner. I asked Lodinyo, "Have these people ever heard the name of Jesus?" He replied that he didn't think so, in that he had never walked through this particular region. He said he had invited a few of the passersby during our sabbatical in the riverbed to join us for discussion around the campfire. I couldn't believe it. Here we were, in the middle of the African wilderness, about to have the privilege and the pressing responsibility of sharing the Gospel.

One by one, the people came and took their places at the campfire. After welcoming them, Lodinyo began speaking in a relaxed, conversational way, although I didn't understand a word he was saying other than the occasional reference to "Yesu." He wasn't preaching. Rather, he was imparting important information. It was a two-way conversation between him and the elders, and on occasion, Lodinyo would pull his head back and laugh as if there was no tomorrow. "What are they saying?" I asked at one particular moment of obvious levity. Lodinyo responded, "They want me to bring this man called Jesus here so they can sit with Him!" He said that they would like to agree with what this man "Yesu" has to say, but in order to make any kind of decision about whether or not to follow him, it would necessitate a face-to-face, sit-down meeting. They wanted to know if he was from Nairobi. The only other possibility would be that he was from Uganda. These are the only two known places in their realm of understanding regarding the expanse of the world. After explaining to them that Jesus was the Son of God, sent briefly to earth to instruct men in the ways of the Father, they asked whether this place called Heaven was near Nairobi!

I realized, with a start, that the story of Jesus is preposterous. In America we are overly familiar with the concept of God becoming man, and arriving on earth in the usual way as a baby. We don't even blink at the notion of a virgin mother. We accept it as reasonable when Jesus, as a young man, preaches the polar opposite to secular understandings, hangs out with the worst sectors of society, then hand-picks 12 uneducated and unlikely men to be the band of brothers responsible for spreading His unorthodox teachings. After He is unceremoniously killed and buried, we accept on faith that He arose for a few last words before ascending to heaven, leaving behind His powerful spirit to guide our lives. What rational mind would simply "accept" these tales as truth? The questions layered themselves in my mind, and I was struck with the enormous "leap" required for those who had never heard any of this before.

Lodinyo turned to me and said, "Now comes the hard part. I need to tell them about sin." He went on to warn me that this bedraggled crowd would (at least initially) be antagonistic towards any mention of their being sinners. Lodinyo reiterated that in the Pokot culture, there are four serious sins: killing another Pokot intentionally, witchcraft, stealing, and adultery. The restitution for committing one of these sins is serious and can be death. With that as background, the men in particular were extremely agitated when Lodinyo explained that Jesus died for our sins. The question, "Who among us has sinned?" elicited both shock and indignation. Their response: "Point to him who has sinned, and we will deal with the problem directly."

"So what do you do now?" I asked Lodinyo, who was doing a great job of suppressing an obvious inner grin. He went on to effectively explain that sins are transmitted through the blood of our fathers, their fathers, tracing back all the way to the first Pokot. These people certainly know a lot about blood! They nodded their heads, though dubiously, as Lodinyo completed his own version of the *Sermon on the Mount*. I can't recall anyone ever speaking about Jesus with such authority. Then Lodinyo turned to me and said, "Close the session with a prayer." He interpreted. Although my prayer was authentic and straight from the heart, I nevertheless grappled mightily with words and concepts that are so readily accepted and understood in Western culture, realizing that probably most of what I was saying seemed like gibberish to these people. Relying on God's promise to turn my "groans" into comprehensible prayers, we left the group.

I was nearly bursting with anticipation to find out what kind of reaction the people had to their inaugural introduction to Jesus. "So what did they say?" I asked Lodinyo. "They were very interested in this man Jesus," he replied. "Did they accept what you had to say about Him?" Lodinyo looked at me with a patronizing smile and said, "It doesn't work that way. Did it work that way for you?" With a start, I realized that it hadn't. Knowing Jesus had been a long process for me, and a journey that is continuing still. Lodinyo went on to explain, " Over the next few weeks, they will discuss among themselves what we have said. They will talk little of anything else. They will converse, dissect, agree, argue, and discuss some more. In three or four weeks, I will return along this same route to be with them."

What I was really interested in was the previously unspoken question, "Do they believe in Jesus?" I was raised as a Christian to think that, in order for the world to be reconciled to God, people need to hear the "Good News" of Jesus and accept Him in order to be "saved." Lodinyo was grinning from ear to ear as he said, "I told you, it doesn't work that way!" As I shared with Lodinyo my sense of enormous responsibility for being the very first messenger of Jesus, he said, "Ward, we've done our part. We've lifted up His name." I was then stunned by the profound reality of what he said. "The job now belongs to the Holy Spirit! When I return, it will be a very happy time. The Holy Spirit will have been working long and hard!"

Then Lodinyo asked, "How do you defend a lion?" After seeing my questioning look, he went on to say, "Do you hold the lion? Protect him? No, of course not. A lion protects himself. You don't need to. It's the same with the Holy Spirit. Just let Him out and He will do the job!"

I realized a truth with startling clarity: in our society we have become dependent upon people and things to provide purpose and direction for our lives. Because of this I had innocently, yet nevertheless definitely, usurped the dominion and authority of God to be responsible for any human transformation. That transformation can only come from a changed heart. And only God can change a heart.

Lodinyo told me that the gospels have brought many of his people together and transformed them into remarkable companies of faith. It made me think of Jesus talking about himself as the Good Shepherd in John 10:16: *I have other sheep that are not of this sheep pen. I must bring them also. They too will listen to my voice and there shall be one flock and one Shepherd.* I believe He was speaking of my new friends in the remote hills and valleys of West Pokot.

That night, my tent fly wasn't needed, affording me a spectacular painted canvas of endless stars and promised galaxies as distant as this place seemed. The dark outline of the mountain that separates this valley from the rest of this world loomed like a magnificent, ancient time machine.

As I lay in my sleeping bag, I reflected upon the day, a day filled with nothing to do and no place to go. I realized with a jolt, that in the process of doing nothing, I actually had the most profound experience of the trip. I connected with people and learned about their lives. I experienced everyday life, walking with the animals and sitting in the riverbed. I asked a lot of questions and received insightful answers. I learned about poverty in a whole new context. Perhaps most importantly, I saw how the Spirit works. Jesus' instruction, "Lift up My name, and I will attract men," became wonderfully real. I experienced the joy as well as the life itself that rain brings. I saw despair and hopelessness. I saw great courage and strength. I saw overwhelming needs and great ingenuity and adaptability. I was both an object of curiosity and a welcomed foreigner in a community only seldom visited. We talked, napped, read Scripture, and dreamed. Dreams speak to the heart, and they certainly spoke to mine. In retrospect, it was on the day we stopped moving across the land that God was able to speak to me with the greatest clarity.

As the wisps of fragrant smoke wafted across me from the nearly exhausted coals, I said a silent prayer of great thanks, and with a peaceful heart, fell quickly into the darkness of another long and deep sleep.

# CHAPTER 7

# Crossing the Ridge

*The best way out is always through.*
—*Robert Frost*

Aloud and nasty flatulent blast from one of our camel co-inhabitants rudely awakened me at daybreak. Following that startling and unconventional clock alarm, I knew there was no way to snooze. I was again treated to a steaming cup of coffee as we packed up our few provisions for what would be our toughest walk yet. Over the next two days we would be climbing out of this canyon over a 3,000-foot ridge carrying our water for the remaining 23 miles to Mbaro, which was the rendezvous point with the helicopter. We estimated the distance to our first night's layover at Lopet to be 12 miles, and set out at daybreak to avoid having to walk during the scorching heat of the day. As I scanned the endless vista of expanse from our homestead in Domongoria's animal corral, there wasn't a trace of wind. I prayed for strength and endurance for what I knew would be the greatest test of our journey.

As promised, we stopped by the ravine to visit Cheptilak and her four children. We heard their greetings as we approached their homestead. She had three youngsters in addition to the baby on her back. The children were severely emaciated, and had protruded bellies, which are a result of malnutrition, and a precursor to starvation. Lodinyo explained to me that given the fact that the family had no animals for blood, they were on the edge of starvation. Had Cheptilak not encountered us along the riverbank, they would have had no prospects for relief. Wanting to do something to help, I broke apart the protein bars I had been holding in reserve, and Lodinyo fed a small portion to each of the children. After consulting with "Dr. James," Lodinyo left behind an additional ten bars. He instructed Cheptilak to slowly and methodically feed each child over the next seven days, the youngest one in particular, who was in the worst shape.

I took Lodinyo quietly aside and asked what we might be able to do for the people in this valley. Although the rains had just started to fall, it would be at least one month before there would be any vegetation to restore the livestock to former strength so they could again be able to give milk. We decided on a simple plan. Through the community of faith that Lodinyo is establishing in West Pokot, I could anonymously make arrangements for fifty 90-kilo bags of maize to be delivered to Kiwawa. The bags could then be picked up by men from the community who would come with donkeys and camels. This would meet the needs of the community during what promised to be an extremely difficult two months. It would be a much-needed "cup of cold water" to these friends.

I don't know if I did the right thing. It could be argued that people who have never been introduced to help of any kind have the blessing of never having become dependent on anyone. Nevertheless, I was overwhelmed by the enormity of the need and felt no option other than to respond, assuring the continued survival of these people. I recollected the words of Bob Sieple: "If we know something is wrong, we are accountable for that knowledge. We are accountable for what we know. If we can do something about it, we are also responsible.

Accountable knowledge allows for pity. Mercy demands responsible action."

As we were walking away from this clearly desperate family, Lodinyo said to me, "Wardo, so how do you feel?" I responded that I felt strong from our previous day of total rest, and felt up to the challenge of the physically difficult day we were facing. "That's not what I meant," said Lodinyo. "I want you to tell me clearly, how does your heart feel?" When I looked at him questioningly, he went on to say, "I'm wondering how you feel now that you have just saved a human life." I was dumbfounded and deeply troubled. I had done absolutely nothing extraordinary, other than to have been in the right place at the right time with the right resources.

Rather than being elated at the notion of saving a life, I was deeply troubled by the countless number of ravines throughout the surrounding hills that held unspoken stories of starvation, misery, and death. There are no roads, and people are cut off from civilization as we know it. Thus any cries for relief go unheard and unanswered. I had always thought of famine and starvation taking place among large groups of refugees en route to huge feeding camps set up in central locations. This was different. Small families, living independent and remote lives deep in the canyons and hills of Northwest Kenya, were quietly and anonymously dying. The rains don't come. The animals die. Then the people die. One day they are there, and the next day they are gone. Their makeshift, nomadic homes soon fall into disrepair, eventually becoming a lifeless part of the landscape.

Some may say that this is nature's cycle. Some may say that this is a perfect example of the survival of the fittest and a way for nature to keep check on population growth. The truth is people don't die in groups, as statistics would have us believe. Statistics do a cruel injustice to individuals by batching them in numbers, thus obscuring the very real lives being lost and the individual wakes of agony being created. I need to say with all the conviction I can muster that when faced with human lives as pure and as hard fought for as these are, it is every bit a tragedy for them to die as it is for our own beloved sons and daughters in America to die. To negotiate any difference in terms of loss, grief, or importance is a travesty.

As I continued to ponder Lodinyo's question, I reflected that it was indeed Lodinyo who had saved their lives by making arrangements for our trip in this most remote of regions. I then reflected that perhaps it was World Vision that had saved these lives, since their presence in West Pokot was instrumental in creating the opportunity for us to visit. I then reflected that the saving of these lives could clearly be attributed to Dr. Arthur Rouner, my friend who originally invited me to come to Africa. This man was paramount in the initial relief work as well as development activities that followed in West Pokot. As I trudged along, it became clear to me that this journey was all about relationships. Unless God decides to resort to lightning bolts and pillars of fire, once again He is forced to use faulty and frail human beings like us to be His ambassadors. My conclusion was that God saved those lives by mysteriously weaving together numerous relationships, connections, events, and experiences designed and orchestrated invisibly behind the scenes. The credit goes to God alone.

The walk got harder. By 9:00 a.m., the sun was already blazing in our faces as we approached the escarpment that would act as the equivalent of a two-hour workout on a StairMaster inside a raging sauna. We made frequent stops, mostly for my benefit. I noticed that although I was doing my best to ration water, I was consuming the lion's share of what little we had. My companions seemed to hold water like camels; just a small sip would sustain them for hours. I saw just the slightest sheen of sweat on their dust-coated frames. They were in phenomenal physical condition. Any personal trainer back home would be green with envy. Every muscle was clearly de-fined, not for the aesthetics, but purely for function. I thanked God each hour for the gift of having James and Philip to carry the packs. There is absolutely no way I could have climbed that ridge with any kind of a load on my back. However, James and Philip scooted up the crossing trails like Olympic triathletes!

I was struck again by the lack of any discernable path or trail. Our route was a seemingly random combination of turns through valleys and detours around large boulders in the general direction of our destination. Alone, I knew I would be hopelessly lost and thus inevitably doomed. No path or trail means few if any travelers. Aside from the lone traders from Kitale, when people move, they move together as an entire community.

When we finally reached the top of the escarpment, we stopped for lunch, and my friends unwrapped the remnants of the previous night's goat. They quickly lit a campfire and had shish kabobs roasting in five minutes. For the first time, I was sorely tempted by the wafting aroma of cooked meat. I lay down, and my aching joints and muscles were thankful for the sabbatical. Following lunch, my Pokot friends pulled long, two-inch thorns from a nearby Okopko bush and used them as post-lunch toothpicks. I was feeling light-headed, and after observing me for a moment, Lodinyo ordered me to consume one of the remaining power protein bars while we discussed our options. Having traveled approximately 12 miles, we were approaching Lopet, our destination for the day. It was about 1:00 p.m., and the sun was at its hottest. I told Lodinyo, James, and Philip that I felt great and that it might be a good idea to press on past Lopet in order to get closer to our ultimate destination, Mbaro. All three took a quick glance at me and said that if I was up to it, they were all for it! I saw James turn to Lodinyo and whisper, "*Nyakan.*" The others solemnly nodded. The meaning of this word would be explained to me later.

We discovered with dismay that there was a second escarpment wall that would need to be conquered. If anything, this one was steeper and even more littered with boulders and brush. I was starting to lose faith in this adventure. What other surprises lay ahead? Would one of them kill us? Our water supply was nearly as exhausted as I was. If anyone else in our group was concerned, they showed no signs of it. For the first time, I realized that perhaps I couldn't do it. I might not make it. With an enthusiasm that came from my heart and not my mind, we joined hands and chanted *kai kai* (press on). We passed Lopet, which was little more than a few unrelated homesteads with huts and animals. I don't know what I was expecting, but there were going to be no Coke machines here. Despite my frequent sips of filtered water, I was parched. We kept walking. Another steep mountain ridge materialized. Hoping to avoid any more "gross miscalculations," I suggested that we continue our hike as long as possible. I wanted to get closer to the finish line. All I knew was that even if I had to crawl, I wanted to be at the rendezvous point when the helicopter came the following day. Otherwise I wasn't sure I would ever get back.

I was now ignoring the long thorns from the Okopko bushes, and my arms and legs were covered with surface scratches that made intricate patterns on my skin in the collected dust and sweat. I had asked myself (seemingly a thousand times), "What am I doing here?" Now in the fourth day of this incredible journey, I was starting to realize that I probably would never have the answer to that question. Was I here to help encourage Lodinyo? Was I here to provide relief and comfort to that family on the verge of starvation? Was I here for some yet-to-be-revealed higher purpose? Was I here for myself on some type of quasi-spiritual self-inventure? As I pondered these questions under a 100-degree sun, no answers were evident. The questions just kept feeding more questions. I realized that I probably wasn't supposed to know the answers.

The climb up this ridge was even tougher than the first one. I felt myself running out of energy. I was fading fast. I was aware of every step. Each time my foot came down, it would trigger a small explosion of dust, which had turned my legs, socks, and shoes an identical shade of brown. We encountered a family along the way, cooking the remains of a cow that had been killed a few days earlier by a roaming jackal. Again it was evident that nothing is wasted in this part of the world. Oddly this picture was both sad and encouraging to me. With our remaining water quickly diminishing, we decided we needed to keep going all the way to Mbaro. I again heard James mutter the word *nyakan.*

By 3:00 p.m., we had reached the summit of the third ridge and were greeted by a vast expanse of harsh, desolate country-side. I was nearing physical bankruptcy. James and Philip assured Lodinyo and me that Mbaro was just a few hours ahead. The vast landscape, though beautiful, was haunting in its remoteness. All the mountains and valleys looked the same. I realized that the picture I was looking at hadn't changed for centuries. I had no idea how the helicopter pilot would be able to discern any sign of settlement or how he could possibly find me. I secretly moaned about that.

Around 6:00 p.m., we finally reached Mbaro. I was literally stumbling now. I felt wasted and emaciated, and supposed I looked even worse. Nevertheless, I was flooded with a sense of accomplishment. I had made it. The helicopter coming no longer seemed important. Finishing the race was reward enough. We had traveled 56 kilometers over two mountain ranges. The people of the community were amazed that someone other than a Pokot had closed that loop. As Lodinyo addressed the 50 or so villagers, I started feeling faint. My head was swimming and my legs were like rubber. Lodinyo walked me over to one of the grass huts. I lay down with my head on the dirt, and in a moment was unconscious.

After what seemed like forever, I awoke to the setting sun. Lodinyo later told me that they had been more than a little concerned, and had made frequent visits to check my breathing and pulse. Lodinyo would later confess to me that he had told the others that he thought I might be "finished," which, in Pokot terms, means "no longer being among the living." Needless to say, they were eager and happy to welcome me back. Preparations were being made for yet another celebratory goat feast. Our traveling group gathered for our daily sharing from the Bible, and I don't think I have ever said a more earnest prayer of thanksgiving.

At a specially convened meeting of the Pokot elders later that day, the title of *nyakan* was bestowed on me, and I finally learned the meaning of that strange word James had uttered earlier in the day. It denotes "a brave man who faces the unknown, with only faith in God." In the eyes of the Pokot, my completion of the five-day hike through the arid hills, dried-up riverbeds, and rocky terrain earned me the honor. The nobility of anything I had done was lost on me. I had merely walked, or rather stumbled along awkwardly, with people whom I had grown to love and respect. I nevertheless felt honored to be held in high esteem by the elders and to have been warmly embraced by them. I can honestly say that any past physical successes I may have had pale beside the sense of satisfaction this journey gave me. It may singularly have been the most difficult thing I've ever done.

My feelings were tempered somewhat by the realization that if I had known in advance the precise conditions and demands of the journey, I probably wouldn't have gone. But any negative thoughts were overshadowed by the tremendous conviction that for these five days of my life I was precisely at the time and place I was supposed to be. As the cooking fires were reduced to small piles of crimson embers, I realized that the sights, smells, and emotions that just a few days ago had been extraordinary were now embedded in my heart and soul forever.

This night was different. No shuffling of animal hoofs. There was a small breeze coming up from the west end of the valley. Soft, muffled voices strained through the thin stick walls comprising my shelter. What were they talking about? Sharing stories from a long time ago? Or maybe about this strange white man who had walked into their time and space.

## CHAPTER 8

# The Long Wave Goodbye

*We shall not cease from exploration; the end of our exploring being
to arrive at the place from which we started and know that place for
the first time.*
                                                        —*T.S. Eliot*

I awoke to seemingly the same muffled voices from the night
before. It was just after first dawn and I again realized how life
here revolves in cycles around the sun. When the sun rises, so do
the people; conversely, when the sun disappears at nightfall, so
do the people.

As I lay there, I noticed a small boy peering into my hut.
When I stirred, he bolted. He then cautiously returned, and I
began playing "face games" with him and was ultimately successful in inviting him into my hut. As a gesture of our newfound
friendship, I gave him half of one of the remaining protein bars.
He accepted slowly, but gratefully. He then rushed out the door.
"Just like kids anywhere," I thought. "He'll no doubt be back for
more." A few minutes later, I glanced through the opening of
the hut to see the boy giving the entire portion of his gift to a
small girl, presumably his sister, who was clearly in poor health
and lying on the ground. I wept.

I noticed a long queue outside one of the huts. When I
went to investigate, I found "Dr. James" diagnosing and treating
sick young children. I was again struck by the prospective pa-
tients' lack of any semblance of "pushing and shoving," though
they were clearly in desperate need. There was still a substantial

line when James inevitably ran out of medical supplies. I was able to (at least briefly) restock him with the contents of my emergency medical kit, but the vast needs far outweighed his scant ability to address them. Once the supplies were exhausted, the untreated mothers and children left the hut with no complaints, let alone frustration or anger, and there was not so much as a whimper from the sick children. I wept again.

We were now somewhat back in the realm of "civilization." I knew that my departure would be by helicopter at Eldoret, followed by flight connections at Nairobi, Kenya, and on to Addis Ababa in Ethiopia. I realized with a start that I would have no access to a sink, let alone a shower, to make myself presentable. I gathered a crowd as I stooped over a carved out wooden bowl and attempted to wash five days worth of sweat out of my shirt. I was then presented with a bowl of water that resembled that of the "fresh-water spring," which I was able to use for a quick shower  in the privacy of a small grove of trees. Although I didn't have a mirror, I assumed that despite my best efforts, I was a pretty sad picture.

Lodinyo informed me that in the community there were only a few warriors with the designation *nyakan*, and he wanted to introduce me to one of them. When I met the man, I commented on the numerous tattoo-like marks on his right arm and chest. Lodinyo explained to me that the marks signify that he has killed at least one person. I made the point to distinguish the differences in how we acquired our credentials!

While I still had my doubts about the helicopter finding this speck of a community, I was no longer afraid. If it came, it came. If it didn't, I knew I could survive. Rather than feeling total joy at having this experience behind me, I was saddened by its impending end. I knew in many ways, both large and small, that I had changed. I wasn't sure how or why, but in my soul I knew I once again owed a tremendous debt of gratitude to Africa.

A few of the children who had been brought to "Dr. James" were clearly in bad shape. James distributed the balance of the protein bars based on extremity of need. Lodinyo promised to return with more supplies in the weeks following our visit. He expressed an interest in returning the following month with a group of his lay pastors and a choir for a weeklong celebration to lift up the name of Jesus and to "be" with the people. They pressed him for details, and he said that probably 20 of them would come.

Later, Lodinyo laid out a plan for his return. He budgeted the needs for a journey that would involve him, his group of 11 brothers in faith, and the "Kiwawa Flames," a magnificent choir of men and women from the village of Kiwawa. The troupe would travel via Land Rovers, bushwhacking through the rocky landscape that separates Mbaro from the relative civilization in Kiwawa. A critical part of this traveling church are three women —Margaret Nangoria, Knight MaMgwe, and Lodinyo's wife Ruth— who do the packing, cooking, sewing, and attend to other physical needs.

Lodinyo explained that the first day of the weeklong gathering, he and his people would be guests of the community. After that, they would be totally self-supportive so as not to be a burden to the village. The budget was lean. Corn, sugar, tea, cooking oil, a single goat, and fuel for the vehicles were mandatory. When I pressed Lodinyo for a number, he told me that such a gathering (including food, supplies, and transportation) would cost less than 100 U.S. dollars. I remarked that it seemed like a small amount for that many people for five days, and Lodinyo with his customary ear-to-ear grin indicated, "When we travel, we eat most economically!" He also reminded me that, more importantly, while we were away, the Spirit would be working. The "Lion" would be at work.

When it was time to leave, it seemed the entire village accompanied us as we proceeded up the dusty final trail to a cleared out, relatively flat area that would serve as the landing pad for the helicopter. After what seemed like an infinite wait, I heard the thumping rhythm of the rotors, and then saw the helicopter rounding the ridge. We were in hopes that our entire team of five could be airlifted to Kapenguria, but the pilot informed us that he had room only for Lodinyo and me due to weight restrictions. Philip and James didn't seem even to blink at what I considered to be disastrous news.

As I hugged these precious porters and newfound friends, I found myself in tears. They weren't the least bit reticent about retracing our steps back home and were simply grateful to have been able to spend time together and share experiences that they'll never forget. So, up we went in a cloud of dust, Lodinyo and me, on the way to our respective homes. Lodinyo's statement on our family's deck that I had never *really* been to West Pokot and had never *really* been with him had been accurate. As I struggled with my own emotions, and tried to sort through my thoughts and perceptions, I was overwhelmed with thankfulness for Lodinyo and this wonderful African community, who gave me so much.

CHAPTER 9

# The Lion at Work

*Treat the other man's faith gently; it is all he has to believe with.*
*—Henry S. Haskins*

Three weeks after our helicopter exit from Mbaro, Lodinyo did indeed retrace our steps. This time he was accompanied by the "Kiwawa Flames," 11 pastors and the three women who care for the troupe. As Lodinyo promised, the Holy Spirit had been at work! The "Lion" was roaming freely! Mbaro was bursting with energy and spirit.

During the initial return visit, Lodinyo explained that the pastors and other believers ministered one-on-one to those who came with questions and open hearts. They sat together for long periods of time, talking, sharing, and discussing person-to-person or in small groups. Towards the end of the week, the group came together for singing, praying, preaching, and celebrating the Good News that by then had permeated them with the unmistakable presence of the Holy Spirit. It was right out of the book of Acts.

Lodinyo shared with me the fact that only four out of the 13 pastors in the area could read and write. When he first told me this, it seemed like a recipe for misinterpretation and mistakes. I wondered, "How can you preach when you can't read?"

Lodinyo explained that most of the pastors are former warriors who, by virtue of their past bravery and conquests, have earned the trust (and the ear) of the people. Most formerly carried AK-47s under their arms in addition to the traditional stool and walking stick. Lodinyo has replaced AK-47s with the greatest weapon of all, the Bible. Unfortunately, only the New Testament has been translated into the Pokot dialect to date.

The strategy of the illiterate pastors is to go down from the remote hills into the more populated areas and seek out someone who can read. This is usually a young person who has received training through one of the area outpost schools, which are sponsored by various faith-based organizations.

The pastor then gives the Bible to the student and asks him to read to him, urging him to find a place where Jesus or Paul is speaking. He then asks the student to read the entire passage. This is followed by trying to identify one main point or key verse. This gives the pastor a way to prepare a simple sermon. Then the pastor starts asking questions. For example, "What do you think Jesus meant when He said we are to love our enemies?" "What can we learn from this?" "How can this be relevant to our lives?" etc, etc. The passage and subsequent meaning result in an intense interactive dialogue between the pastor and this newfound "student." The pastor then meditates on the words and the message for the balance of the week. Lodinyo likens it to a cow that digests its food very slowly. It's called "ruminating," I told him. "Exactly!" he responded. The pastor "ruminates" and by the end of the week, the lesson is fully digested! "By Sunday, there is always a powerful message! Ward, I tell you, it is the Lion at work!"

Three months after my trip, my good friend, Sharon, told me she was traveling to Kenya with her niece, who is an anthropologist and an agnostic. She had heard about my travels into the unknown of West Pokot and was deeply intrigued. I advised them that it might not be practical to retrace the steps I had taken, given their relatively short itinerary and their lesser appetite for adventure, but I did suggest that they have Lodinyo bushwhack with them to Mbaro, which is where I departed by helicopter. There are no direct roads, but nevertheless the terrain is passable by a four-wheel-drive vehicle.

A few weeks later, back in Minnesota, I encountered Sharon and, somewhat surprisingly, her niece at a Sunday morning church service. Her niece came up to me, and excitedly related the magnificent time they had exploring the outer edges of West Pokot. I asked if the experience had been helpful for her anthropology studies and research. She said she had been intrigued by the culture, but said it wasn't what had made the greatest impact on her. When I asked her what had, her expression changed, and she said, "The church in Mbaro." "But there isn't a church in Mbaro," I replied. "It's only a small village with a clearing just large enough for a helicopter to land." "Well, there's a church there now," she replied. "When we went there last Sunday, more than 250 people were worshipping there."

A few months later, Lodinyo reported that people were now gathering regularly under three huge trees that provided the only real shade in the region. In the morning, they would sit on one side of the tree; in the afternoon they would chase the

shade to the other side. People didn't want to leave the "church," so the Sunday service lasted all day and typically included at least three sermons from Pastor Lodinyo. "Sometimes when it rains," Lodinyo told me, "We postpone our Sunday till another day. But we have to have our Sunday! We find joy under the tree."

A year later, I had the privilege of returning to Mbaro with U.S. businessman Mike Sime and Greg Snell from Kitale. We were amazed at what we saw. We arrived in the late afternoon on a Saturday and were greeted with song and celebration by this new community of faith. Villagers from as far as 25 miles away had begun arriving for Sunday's worship gathering. I was pleased to see that they had reserved my "room," the same hut I had inhabited the year before. At about 8:00 p.m., shortly after the sun had disappeared, the singing began in earnest. It continued until 1:00 a.m.!

Sunday morning we wandered up a rocky path to a spectacular clearing crowned by the three towering trees, which serve as a natural cathedral. The service was scheduled to begin at 1:00 p.m. By 10:30 a.m., there were already 100 or so people gathered in song, to be joined by an endless stream of newcomers from Kasei, Tarakit, Sinjolol, and other surrounding communities. Pastor Daniel would be preaching that day. He arrived around 11:00 a.m., following the 26-mile walk from Kasei that he had begun before dawn. He was joined by pastor Amos, who lives in Mbaro, as well as the ever-present Lodinyo, and they alternated reading from Scripture with accompanying messages and explanations.

As Lodinyo interpreted the message and added his insights, the message was then summarized and turned into beautifully harmonic choruses sung by the entire congregation. This allowed the message to be placed firmly within the memory and hearts of the people, given there are no written transcripts.

About noon, we were startled by the sound of additional voices from afar. Just west of the gathering, there appeared an assembly of approximately 50 villagers from Sinjolol, which lies two hours to the north. They were greeted excitedly and quickly assimilated into the expanded service under the tree. As it turned out, a few women from Sinjolol had previously visited the church. They reported to Lodinyo that after they returned to Sinjolol, a church had been formed there. No building, no organization, no deacons, no pastor. "It just has burst in our community," they told us. They told Lodinyo that they now needed a pastor to bring the Scriptures to them.

At 12:30 p.m., 30 to 40 more worshipers arrived waving palm branches only found in the community of Tarakit at the top of the mountain, four hours off to the south. There was a seamless progression of songs and Scripture, celebrating the presence of God. It was "church" in the true meaning of the word. It was not a show for us. It was a celebration, a magnificent example of worship, gratitude, and prayers for the audience of one—God.

CHAPTER 10

# The Audience of One

*Concentrate on today. Be a today man, not a yesterday man, nor a tomorrow man. Live today. For if you try to live three ways at once— living in worry over the mistakes of yesterday, living tensely about tomorrow, you will be living ineffectively today.*

—*E. Stanley Jones*

The five-day walk with Lodinyo and my Pokot friends may be singularly the most important thing I've done in my life. When I say this to friends and family, they react with skepticism. How could a walk in the middle of nowhere qualify as most important? I think it's because when I moved out in faith towards the unknown like a *nyakan*, God worked powerfully in my life.

The long walk in West Pokot taught me a lot about living in the present. In the places we visited, there was no time to think about the past, and no sense in thinking about the future. I experienced life as it was happening. I was inextricably locked in the present and, ironically, it provided an escape from the frantic pace, countless responsibilities, and endless activities of my daily life back home. I was able to experience much keener spiritual vision and clarity. I developed remarkably close bonds with my new friends as a result of the experiences we shared and the focused time we spent together. I prayed instead of planning. I listened more than I talked. I learned more than I taught.

The purpose of the walk remains a mystery. I'm not sure I will ever know exactly why it happened. Perhaps the trip was meant to be an encouragement to Lodinyo and the people in West Pokot, who face daily trials and frequent tragedies and disasters and who are off the radar screen of the rest of the world. Perhaps the experience was meant to help facilitate emergency food relief to people staring into the abyss of starvation. Perhaps I was supposed to experience living with the "poorest of the poor" as a prelude to subsequent work with those in positions to effect national change. The answer has not yet come to me.

I only know that as I sat with those Pokot elders in the dried up river basin, and was just "being" for an entire day, I was filled with an overwhelming sense that I was supposed to be there, that I was called in some mysterious way to take this walk. I was filled with a corresponding sense of deep, personal peace that the Apostle Paul describes as "a peace that passes all understanding." Perhaps that was reason enough.

# PART TWO

# Chronic Africa

A journalist was invited by friends to travel to Africa. He accepted the invitation, but as the departure date drew nearer, he became more and more apprehensive about the trip. When the day arrived, he went to the airport with every intention of canceling his plane ticket. Though his friends did their best to reason with him, the journalist seemed resolute in his decision. Then a shadow fell across their discussion, and standing tall above them was a holy man with an ancient, pointed beard and long black robes. The holy man addressed the journalist, saying, "I have a word for you from God." The journalist, noticeably shaken by the man's presence, nevertheless asked him to continue. The holy man said, "You will go to Africa—and you will come back with a terrible disease." Hearing this confirmed the journalist's worst fears. The holy man went on to say, "The disease IS Africa. It will be in your blood for the rest of your life. And you will not be able to stay away." With trepidation, the journalist boarded the plane and went to Africa. And went, and went, and went—again, and again, and again.

# Africa

# Introduction

*I have moved from the agony of questions that I cannot answer, to the reality of answers that I cannot escape.* —*Thomas Skinner*

I have a disease. It's in my bones, and it courses through my veins. I am fully infected and show no signs of remission. The disease is Africa.

I love Africa. I am able to recall vivid pictures of Africa: Six-year-old boys leading herds of scrambling goats through winding paths in the bush, the bramble, and the ever-present dust. The sharp odor of the cooking oil and fires mixed with the acrid smoke from the dying coals. The disregard for time in a society untouched by the warp speed of the technical world. The availability of the people for each other. The sense of community woven together tightly by centuries of time-tested customs and traditions. The slowness of the pace, and the absence of distractions, which allow God's presence to be felt in new and powerful ways.

The ancient drumbeats and rhythms echo the fierce struggles that are equaled only by the fierce determination and pride of the people.

My life has been everlastingly changed by a series of 12 journeys that have taken me from remote African valleys unexplored by the outside world to the state houses, now occupied by a new generation of African leaders.

I am not a pastor, a scholar, a diplomat, or an expert on Africa. The chapters that follow are raw and deeply personal reflections of an American businessman whose life has been turned upside down and inside out by Africa.

Indeed, while exploring the heart and soul of Africa, I ended up finding my own.

# CHAPTER 11

# The Shower of Bricks

*Conversion for me was not a Damascus Road experience. I slowly moved into an intellectual acceptance of what my intuition had always known.* —Madeleine L'Engle

Months after my return from the five-day walk with Lodinyo, every casual acquaintance seemed to ask, "So, how did you find yourself smack in the middle of one of the most remote regions of Africa?"

When Africa first showed up on my radar screen, I saw it as a meaningless blip. I had no interest in the remote continent, miles and worlds away from my comfortable life in the U.S. It was the early 1980s, and a prolonged drought in Africa had resulted in widespread famine. People were starving to death by the hundreds each day. Many were collapsing and dying on the long walks to the feeding camps that had been established by world relief agencies. The newspapers gave daily reports on the horrific situation there. But to me, it was just ink on paper. That isn't to say I didn't care. I just had no connection to it. I didn't relate.

I was a well-to-do American, living in my own insulated world. I ran a prosperous business, had a loving and healthy family, lots of friends, and endless opportunities. My life was busy and full. I worked hard and played hard. My schedule was demanding, and my life felt complete. There was no room for the bad news coming out of Africa.

I once heard that when God wants to get your attention, he begins by throwing little pebbles at you. If that doesn't work, He increases the size of the stones. For those who just aren't paying attention, God resorts to bricks. Africa was my brick.

In 1992, on my way out of a Sunday morning church service, my lifelong pastor, Dr. Arthur Rouner, stopped me and asked if I wanted to go to Africa with him. I couldn't believe what he was saying. Africa? He might as well have asked me to go to the moon! Seeing my reaction, he politely said, "Ward, why don't you just pray about it." I looked him squarely in the eye and said, "Arthur, you're the minister, you pray about it. I'll think about it."

Two months later, I found myself in a small airplane on a makeshift, rock-strewn, dirt runway in north central Ethiopia. I couldn't tell you why. The purpose of the trip seemed vague to me. We were supposed to prepare some type of report on the use of funds provided by a number of Twin Cities churches for relief and development efforts facilitated by World Vision in the Antsokia Valley (it had been referred to as the "Valley of Death" during the famine in the mid 1980s). A few hours later on a bumpy dirt road that meandered through the valley and up into a spectacular series of hills, we encountered a little girl.

I left the others and approached her with my camera in tow. She was beautiful. On her back was an impossible load of bamboo sticks, which are used for firewood. I was sure the sticks weighed more than she did. The twine ropes from her burden cut deeply into her heaving chest as she paused and looked back at me with an indefinable expression of fear and surprise. I saw in her an almost fierce determination. Her eyes locked with mine, and somehow I was able to travel through that stare, and connect with her. She was four years old, the same age as my daughter, Sarah. Mentally, I made comparisons. They both possessed a unique, youthful beauty. However, the differences could not have been more profound. The tattered brown rag that served as this little girl's dress was color-coordinated with the soot marks on her neck, as well as the light coat of dust that covered her arms and legs. Her feet were scratched and bruised, and the palms of her hands were coarse from labor. Despite (or maybe because of) the rags, the dust, and the tremendous burden, this little girl carried a sense of dignity and grace that touched me deeply. As I looked into her beautiful midnight brown eyes, I felt her gaze go deeper and bury itself in my soul. I took a photograph of her, and the negative is permanently lodged in my heart. I knew her only as the "girl with the sticks," but she instantly became a part of my future. The first brick had been thrown—and it had brown eyes.

Next, we visited an abandoned series of dilapidated wooden buildings and shelters that had been set up as relief food camps for the starving refugees of the famine in the 1980s. I couldn't help but conjure up images of the specters of human beings full of anguish, misery, and despair, stumbling and staggering up the rocky path that led to this relative haven of basic nourishment and care. I also felt the presence of the ghosts of the countless who didn't make it to the camp. The full weight of the tragedy —the senselessness of people starving to death—pulled like a steamship anchor on my heart. Sure, I had seen the pictures and read the news reports, but now those statistics were coming alive in my heart. Another brick.

As we traveled on, we met surviving family members who told stories about the loved ones they had lost during the famine years. With a painful new awareness, I began to notice the absence of teenagers in the villages we were visiting, and I realized with a chill that few children had survived the famine. Now, nearly a generation was missing.

The day had left me with a lot to absorb. Questions upon questions began flooding my mind. What was I doing here? Why had I come? What was all of this supposed to mean? My thoughts were a kaleidoscope of unsortable emotions. I was a million miles outside my comfort zone—seemingly on a different planet in a different universe. I had never been more deeply moved or confused in my life.

Later that evening around the blazing campfire, I started to feel detached from the group and the mission. Whatever faith I might have had seemed to be slipping away, and I found myself in tears. It was uncharacteristic for me; I very seldom cry. I was embarrassed by this rare show of emotion and did my best to hide my tears from my fellow travelers. Then, somewhat to my own surprise, I found myself uttering a prayer. The stammering expression was directly addressed to God. I said quietly (but aloud), "God, Your name keeps coming up. I don't know why I'm here. I do know that much of what we've been discussing concerns You. I'm not sure I can take much more of this. I want to make a deal. I will surrender to whatever experiences you have in store for me over the next two-and-a-half weeks. If you want to embarrass me, fine. If you want to make me physically or mentally uncomfortable, I'll get through it. If you want me to cry, I will. If you want me to eat lousy food, I'll do it. But I want to make this clear: the deal is for the next two-and-a-half weeks. No more, no less. And then I'll return to my normal life back home."

# Chapter 12

# The New Deal

*Grace fills empty spaces, but it can only enter where there is a void
to receive it, and it is grace itself which makes this void.*
                                                        —*Simone Weil*

The prayer at the campfire hadn't come naturally or easily
for me, but logic dictated the necessity of emotional
surrender if I was going to physically and psychologically survive
the trip. It was clear to me that Africa requires faith, and I
promised to pay close attention to whatever lessons God wanted
me to learn.

At first, the idea of giving up control was frightening to me.
I am by nature a hands-on-the-steering-wheel kind of guy. As the
owner of a small, closely held company, I manage virtually every
aspect of the business. At home, I organize family events and
activities. I find it relatively easy and highly desirable to be in
charge. Now, in this new place, everything was different. Though
it should have been obvious to me, what took me by surprise is
that once I had relinquished the driver's seat, I was able to sit
back and just ride. I could focus on the present, make the most
of each experience, and just "be." At the same time, I knew I
needed to brace myself for what was ahead.

In Masaka, Uganda, which is believed by many to be the
birthplace of AIDS, we visited a family living in a small straw and
mud house. Before entering the house, we were told that the

husband had died of AIDS a few months earlier and that the mother was in the final vestiges of the horrific disease. We were greeted at the door by the woman's 12-year-old daughter and three younger siblings. The mother lay on a straw mat on the floor of the one-room dwelling. There was an active wasps' nest on the ceiling above her head. Her body had shrunk to unimaginable proportions, and despite rheumy eyes, she projected an almost heroic sense of courage, pride, and dignity. She was dying. The 12-year-old had just returned from a neighbor's field, where she had worked all day to pay off the debt of the previous day's dinner. From the mat on the floor, the mother gave her instructions on chores and infant care; she would continue giving them until she, too, died in front of her children, just as their father did months before.

In a remote region of northwest Kenya, along the Ugandan border, I thought at the time I was witnessing the very far edge of the civilized world. Poverty was defined on an entirely new scale. Now the pictures I had only seen in magazines or newspapers of children with distended stomachs and eyes covered with flies became excruciatingly real. I became acquainted with people living on the very edge of survival itself. Their "givens" were a harsh and unforgiving climate, no assets, and no enterprise. To me, they represented a 180-degree turn back in time to the nomadic communities described in the Bible.

As I sat on the top of a hill with one of the World Vision workers, I noticed that the hot winds at this end of the great Rift Valley blew strong and constantly during our entire visit. Pondering this, I turned and asked, "Why don't you have windpumps here to provide water for your communities?" He turned to me with a sparkle in his eye and said, "Why don't we have a Macy's Department Store? It's all about resources." That thought stayed with me throughout the visit, and I became increasingly aware that the biggest challenge facing this community and all those like it in rural Africa is the lack of water. Diseases like typhoid and cholera, which have been eradicated and forgotten in America, are still killers here. Children go blind from the lack of clean water with which to wash their faces and remove the larvae left by the hoards of flies. It's commonplace for women to walk up to 20 miles roundtrip each day to collect the water necessary to support their families and their livestock.

I visited the worst parts of the slums of Soweto in Johannesburg, and the Mathare Valley in Kenya, and witnessed firsthand the meaning of hopelessness. I saw people living in desperation, largely unnoticed by the rest of the world.

I saw an abundance of soul in the obvious lack of provision. I saw the deep richness of relationships and community in neighborhoods lacking even the very barest of resources.

I saw the great wealth of community, family, and friendships amid abject material poverty.

I saw the ability of God to finally invade my own heart. People have asked me, "Do you really think you needed to go half way around the world to Africa to find God?" For me, the answer was "yes." I needed to get that far away from the familiar.

Without my knowing it, I had methodically become infected with the disease called Africa. There had been no black-robed messenger at the airport to warn me.

## CHAPTER 13

# Jousting with Windmills

*When you come to the fork in the road, take it.* —*Yogi Berra*

I returned from that first trip to Africa not only infected, but contagious. I was ablaze with passion, and wanted to actively address the overwhelming needs I had witnessed. I wanted to make a meaningful contribution toward alleviating at least some of the misery and suffering we had seen.

By far the most difficult aspect of returning home was the apathy I encountered from friends and acquaintances toward this remarkable life-changing journey. Why didn't anybody understand? It wasn't as though no one asked about it—plenty of people did. But whenever I started responding to their questions, I found people glancing at their watches with body language clearly begging for release from my exotic travelogue. People wanted a "nutshell" version that, at the time, I found impossible to deliver. I was both hurt and discouraged, and my soul wanted to cry out to them, "Why can't you see it? Why don't you care? Are you so caught up in the madness of a society where meaningful relationships and a sense of community have been forfeited to the quest for material comforts and personal security?"

Thankfully, I was able to quickly abandon this sanctimonious school of thought. A brief personal inventory reminded me that, just months before, I had consulted my own watch many times and nearly fallen asleep during a discussion with travelers who had taken a nearly identical trip! My zeal and newfound "wisdom" was causing people to no doubt silently think, "Well, if you like Africa so much, why don't you just pick up and move there?"

A few weeks after my return, I gathered in the conference room of my company with ten of my best and most trusted friends in the Twin Cities business community, with an invitation for me to "tell my story." I'm sure that most of them came out of a sense of respect for me, rather than a compelling desire to hear about my trip. I'll never forget how each one entered the room somewhat reluctantly and sat with arms crossed, looking expectantly at me. They had all come with checkbooks in hand, anticipating responding to yet another fundraising effort (for which I had become somewhat infamous). I started the discussion by explaining that I didn't want their money, but rather I wanted their hearts. I wanted them to hear an unabridged account of an experience that had profoundly shaken every concept I had previously held, and had given me a brand new awareness of a world that previously, for me, hadn't existed. I spoke not only about the crushing needs and agony of a part of the world with no safety nets, but also about how this expanded view of humanity had profoundly humbled me. Whereas before the trip, I was at the "top of my game," I now found myself with far more questions than answers, with the biggest one being, "What else don't I know anything about?"

Talking with these friends and business leaders was a big risk for me. I knew it then, but was compelled to take it. I closed our time together by sharing my vision and dream for developing windpumps in Northwest Kenya. Not surprisingly, one of my best friends, Rich Cammack, immediately put his hand in the air and said, "Whatever you're going to do, count me in." I'm sure that a few left that day thinking, "Ward's really gone off the deep end this time." In retrospect, they probably were right.

As a result of my meeting with this small group, substantial funding was secured. I went back to World Vision, an international, interdenominational relief and development organization, with a commitment to build a windpump in the far-away community that had impacted me so immensely.

A few months later at an outdoor bistro in Cannes, France, I sat drinking coffee with a friend, Kevin Burke, a businessman from Los Angeles. While in Africa, I had placed on my wrist three crudely crafted copper and iron bracelets from the places we had been, making a promise to myself never to take them off. I guess I wanted or needed an external reminder of my experiences for fear that they might eventually fade from my memory. Looking at the bracelets, Kevin joked that perhaps I was either "coming out of the closet" or at least becoming more "Californian." However, as I started sharing my stories of Africa, he became increasingly focused and never once glanced at his watch. I will never forget the intensity of his interest and the depth of that discussion. His final question floored me. He quietly said, "Will you take me to Africa?" My response was an immediate "no." I wasn't going back to Africa. That was never part of the plan. The notion was absurd. I had already been to Africa. No way! But my words were falling on deaf ears. Kevin wasn't about to give up. He looked at me intently and said, "I want to go to Africa and I want you to take me. "

When I got back to Minnesota, I put together a meeting of those who had committed to the windpump project. I laughingly recounted to the group my meeting with Kevin and his actually wanting to go to Africa. There wasn't any laughter. After a few moments, Rich Cammack turned to me and said, "I want to go, too." To my amazement, others followed.

I was reluctant to go back. Fundraising was one thing, but revisiting Africa was a completely different deal. I was becoming increasingly comfortable with my experiences there, but the notion of returning with a group of expectant business peers was uncomfortable at best and paralyzing at worst. God was opening up another door. Yet at the time, this one seemed more like an elevator shaft.

I kept waiting and secretly hoping for some good reasons not to go back. The trip had changed my life and perspectives in many ways, but the prospect of returning just a year later seemed redundant. I met with Arthur Rouner, who had led our first group, as well as 15 previous groups, to various destinations in East Africa. He affirmed the idea of a windpump team excursion to Africa as a wonderful opportunity and agreed to be part of it. When I went to World Vision with this proposal, I was given a green light to proceed. Doors were opened. The die was cast. I would be returning to Africa.

In the ensuing months, I met frequently with Arthur, and in a moment of weakness (in retrospect, strength) promised to go with him to India for ten days prior to meeting the Windpump Team in Nairobi, Kenya. I will never forget standing in the Bombay airport at 3:30 in the morning, about to get on a plane to Nairobi. I had just realized that my committed group of American friends was actually airborne en route to Kenya. They were bound for Africa solely (or so I feared) as a result of my influence. At that moment I felt it was all a terrible mistake. Memories of the hardships I had endured during the first trip came flooding back. It hadn't been fun at all. Often, it had been either extremely difficult or excruciatingly boring. My friends had left their families and their businesses to travel halfway across the world, and I was 100 percent convinced that, even though they had asked me to take them, they were going to hate it. I could almost hear their certain refrain; "Brehm, we would have been happy to have written a check toward these windpumps, but why did you make us come?"

In a corner of the Bombay Airport, Arthur and I had miraculously found a tiny little kiosk that served espresso in the middle of the night. As we sat there quietly, I turned to him and somewhat innocently asked, "Have you ever brought anyone with you to Africa who hated the experience?" Thankfully, he didn't answer right away. But after a few minutes and careful thought, he responded, "No. I don't think I can recall a single instance where a life has not been profoundly affected." The conviction of his words filled me with quiet confidence and affirmation. I had forgotten that God was behind the steering wheel—and it wouldn't be the first time, or the last.

CHAPTER 14

# This wasn't on my Itinerary!

*I prayed, "Lord, how am I supposed to do my job with all these distractions?" The answer came, "These distractions are your job."*

—*Henri Nouwen*

Being a highly organized, controlling, type-A businessman, my new role as a logistics leader for a team in Africa seemed a perfect fit for me. The problem is that, particularly in Africa, things usually don't go according to plan. In fact, things go wrong—a lot.

On my first trip to Africa, we had originally been scheduled to take the *Lunatic Express*, an infamous railroad connecting Nairobi to Mombassa, a major port for Kenya, which lies along the beautiful eastern coast of the Indian Ocean. Despite our best American efforts in making arrangements for the appropriate sleeping car compartment tickets, we weren't able to get confirmation. We were frustrated, but for me, a take-charge business guy, it was a call to action. "I'll handle it," I said as I hailed a taxi to the ticket office. Sure enough, our names appeared nowhere. At the time, there were no computers in the train station's ticket office. The records were hand-entered ledgers, and despite my expressed frustration, our names couldn't be found on the list of confirmed passengers. The train was fully booked. We weren't going to Mombassa.

Having failed in my efforts, I returned somewhat sheepishly to the hotel and reported the bad news to the group. The time in Mombassa had been planned as a beautiful and relaxing diversion to an otherwise difficult trip. We amended our plans and traveled instead to Arusha, Tanzania, and there established some relationships and friendships that endure to this day. Three days later, we learned that the train we had hoped to take to Mombassa had gone off the tracks in the middle of the night during the return trip, killing more than 80 people and crippling and wounding countless others. The "what ifs" still haunt me to this day.

One of the most grueling experiences I had on my second trip was an 11-hour drive from Lowoi in West Pokot to Nairobi. I felt no need to share this ordeal with my new traveling companions. In working with World Vision on our itinerary, I was insistent (ad nauseum) that we would be chartering a plane for this leg of the trip. Upon arriving, I was informed that the plans had changed. There would be no plane to West Pokot. The farthest we could fly was Kitale, approximately six hours south of our windpump site. To say the least, I wasn't happy. Our whole itinerary was getting messed up! Trying hard, but unsuccessfully, to hide my frustration and aggravation from the team, I informed them of the change—and was met with nothing more than shrugging shoulders. They were novices! They didn't understand! In Northwest Kenya, roads, as we know them, do not exist. We would be traveling mostly on dried-up riverbeds. If only they knew.

Things got worse. When we arrived in Kitale, we were met by the World Vision director, who informed us that one of the World Vision vehicles had broken down. He meant really broken down—out of commission for at least two weeks. Our team's collective gaze focused on the remaining vehicle, which was designed for six passengers. We numbered 11! With our packs and gear, it seemed impossible. Clearly it was a "No way, Jose" situation. But as often happens in Africa, it was the only way. With a few grumbles, but mostly silence, we all jammed into the Land Cruiser. The packs and supplies were crammed between bodies and into every nook and cranny of available space. When one team member adroitly began lowering the windows, the driver responded, "We will need to keep the windows closed.

Lots of dust." It was 100 degrees and we all wordlessly asked ourselves if we had used enough deodorant! As we rolled out of Kitale, the silence of the group spoke loudly. Just when it seemed as though we were all on the verge of a claustrophobic breakdown, Rich Cammack turned as best he could toward Arthur and asked, "Do you have any thoughts about the devil?"

I wish the following four hours had been recorded or transcribed! Arthur's words on the reality, the power, and the resulting challenges that we would face in life due to the forces of evil were captured by ten hearts. It may well have been the finest sermon of his long and distinguished career. The time flew. And it wouldn't be the last time that "my plans" were rudely interrupted by logistical mishaps that provided lessons far greater than any I could have orchestrated.

This phenomenon repeated itself time and time again. By things not working out, they ended up working perfectly. During the third journey with a group supporting the windpumps, we had chartered a plane from Entebbe, Uganda, to Tarangire, Tanzania, with a customs check and refueling at Mwanza which lies on the southern shore of Lake Victoria. Anticipating the way things often work in Africa, our pilot had confirmed the day before that there was gasoline reserved for our refueling the next day. When we landed, no gas was available. The Mwanza airport was another experience I'd hoped to spare the others; the dimly lit waiting room was a far, far cry from an airline perks club. It was apparent to all that it would be our residence for the unforeseeable future. The tented camp at Tarangire, complete with a promise of a hot shower, an African feast, and bonfire was quickly replaced with the prospect of a dinner of ancient-looking candy bars and warm pop, and a respite on weathered Naugahyde couches of a pre-colonial era.

The emotions of panic, anger, frustration, and ultimately depression made the rounds among the members of our group. Out of that sense of quiet desperation, someone suggested that we do our daily Bible study. We read I Corinthians 12, which centered on spiritual gifts. We talked about the importance of recognizing our individual gifts, as well as the gifts of others, and bringing them into harmony. Our team had expanded to include Mike Harries, the inventor and manufacturer of the windpumps we had purchased in Kenya, and Tekle Selassie, an extraordinary spiritual mentor. The discussion with Arthur, Tekle, and Mike took us to depths of spiritual insight that none of us had ever fathomed. It was one of the most mind-stretching, soul-expanding experiences I have ever had. The Spirit was in our midst. Our miserable surroundings seemed to disappear. Our complaints were totally mute; our sense of time, distorted. And when, after more than three hours, the Book was closed, we sat in stunned silence. At that precise moment, we were brought back to reality by the pilot, who walked in and informed us that fuel had been found and we were ready to fly.

We made it to Tarangire. We had hot showers, an African feast, and an evening bonfire. But had we not had the aggravating delay at Mwanza, we would have been robbed of one of the high spiritual times of the journey.

# CHAPTER 15

# Penlights and Passion

*And I said to the man who stood at the gate of the year, "Give me a light that I may tread safely into the unknown." And he replied, "Go out into the darkness and put your hand into the hand of God. That shall be to you better than light and safer than a known way.*
*—Louise Haskins*

After the first Windpump Team traveled to West Pokot, the windpump project took on an energy of its own. And, much to my surprise, I continued leading groups to Africa annually. Thanks to that initial company of willing guys with open minds and great hearts, good things happened. Windpumps were built in three Kenyan communities—Kiwawa, Lowoi, and Parakor—and residents finally had clean, safe water close by. An agreement was struck with the elders of those communities. It was to work this way: (1) the windpump team would provide the funds and the technical requirements; (2) the village would sell one goat per family to cover costs for maintenance and repairs; and (3) God would provide the wind.

From the beginning, World Vision had warned us that West Pokot was a difficult place for development. The people are historically pastoralists and nomads, with the primary emphasis being on finding water for their cattle. For nearly two decades, a dependency on aid had been growing.

On my third visit to West Pokot, I received a tremendous insight into the dynamics of dependency. One of the windpumps had broken, and the elders were furious that the blades had remained motionless for two months. "Why haven't you fixed it?" the elders asked us. My Ethiopian traveling companion, Tekle Selassie, responded loudly and angrily, "How can you treat your guests this way? How can you shirk responsibility for this tremendous asset that was given to your community? These friends from America have no shortage of water back home. This isn't their windpump. This is yours." Referring to the original agreement, he went on to say, "These friends have done their part, but you, in turn, have done nothing." I can honestly say that I was more than a little apprehensive that these "friends" could quickly be turned into enemies based on Tekle's message and the passion with which it was delivered. The elders then turned their backs on us and began discussing among themselves what had been said. I nervously eyed the spears that lay at their feet, and quietly prayed that they wouldn't come into play. A few minutes later, an old man designated as the spokesman slowly rose and said, "We want you to know two things, and both are very important: The first is that we agree with everything you have said. The second is that it's the first time we have ever understood it."

The elder went on to say that over the past 30 years, when white men came, they helped. Beginning with what they referred to as "the difficult days" of famine in the 1980s across most of East Africa, many people came and helped in any way they could. "They did things for us. We looked to them for help, and they provided it. What you are now saying is, for us, a new way forward."

One of the most exhilarating experiences I've had in Africa came during a subsequent visit to West Pokot with Senator Dave Durenberger. On an earlier trip, women from the village of

Parakor had approached our group and asked if we would be willing to provide them with a diesel-powered maize mill. We had asked many questions regarding fuel accessibility and maintenance, and were encouraged by the very strategic and intentional thinking of these women. The mill would be a business, and a portion of the profits would be set aside for maintenance and emergency repairs as well as fuel, which could be purchased and transported by World Vision. Recalling what the elders had said regarding "white people helping," we responded that we would be willing to help them help themselves. A deal was struck. They would need to raise one-half of the total approximate cost of $5,000. I distinctly remember thinking this would be a miracle of mountain-moving proportions, given the lack of any visible commerce or resources, but we agreed and shook hands. A few months before this trip, I received word that the women had indeed met their goal by collecting their share of the money. It had taken them two-and-a-half years, but they had done it! We forwarded our matching funds, and when our group arrived, we were led to the village for the celebratory ribbon cutting. Ever the politician, Senator Durenberger enthusiastically embraced his role as ribbon cutter. The celebration included hundreds of community residents and friends from the surrounding hills.

As it turned out, this wasn't the inaugural for the mill. The women had been using it for the previous month and a half. Towards the end of the grand opening ceremonies, out of the corner of my eye, I noticed an elderly woman with rheumy eyes and a frame bent over from a life of hard labor walking towards our group. She approached Sam Poghisio, my Pokot friend who is a member of the Kenyan National Parliament in Nairobi. I watched as the woman whispered quietly in Sam's ear, and then presented him with a hand-woven basket overflowing with colorful Kenya Schillings. It appeared to be, and probably was, a fortune!

Sam came back to us with an emotional expression on his face that was hard to define. He then told us what the woman had said. It turned out that another community in the surrounding hills had fallen upon hard times. The women from that village had approached the Parakor women to find out about their new maize mill. They were hopeful that they might be able to have one of their own. In response, the women of Parakor used the mill for the month and a half prior to our arrival, and dedicated its profits to establish "seed capital" for their sisters to

the north. They wanted no recognition. They wanted no reward. They just wanted to extend a helping hand to those with similar needs. I couldn't help thinking of the Bible story where the woman put all she had—two copper pennies—in the offering plate.

As time went by, Africa became more and more a part of my everyday life. It seemed I was always making plans for the next trip, and drafting the next team members. I wondered where it all was leading, and what it meant in the scheme of things. I clearly remember a conversation I had with my friend, John Cionca. I explained my dilemma in trying to figure out God's plan for me—the next assignment, the big "To Do" list. I talked about my growing frustration with God for not providing me with "the big picture" so I could get about completing it. John only smiled. He said, "Ward, what you're asking is for God to turn on the search lights and illuminate His plan for you. That's not what He does. God only gives each of us a pen flashlight—so we have just enough light to take the next step."

I have had a very difficult time taming my exuberance for Africa. Africa changed my life and allowed me to see God in a totally new light and in an incredibly personal way. I love the people, who seemingly have very little, yet possess so much in the way of faith, relationships, and presence. I love the pace: nobody tripping over anyone else to be first in line; schedules flexible enough to accommodate the hidden treasure of each day. I love the scenery: wide-open vistas and long views of amazing beauty and a pristine retrospect to life the way it may have been in our own "Wild West" days just 150 years ago. I love Africa, and have never been shy about sharing that love with others.

One day I was sitting with my friend Wheelock Whitney, talking about my most recent trip to Africa. As I was going on and on about the wondrous adventures and spiritual insights, as well as the travails of people facing incomprehensible needs, he gently put his hand over mine and said somewhat brusquely, "Ward, I know what you're trying to do, and it's not going to work."

"I don't know what you're talking about," I replied defensively and with a bit of an edge. "I'm not trying to do anything but just tell you about my trip."

"That's not true, Ward. What you're really trying to do is get me to be passionate about Africa. I'm passionate about many things. I'm passionate about alleviating alcohol and chemical abuse. I'm passionate about Minnesota State politics. I'm passionate about my children and grandchildren. But I'll never be passionate about Africa. I also suspect that somewhere in that tiny brain of yours, you're entertaining the thought of convincing me to go to Africa. It's not going to happen."

I did my best to cover any visible traces of disappointment, but apparently was not successful. Wheelock went on to say, "Ward, although I will never be passionate about Africa, there is one other thing that I can be extremely passionate about. And that is *your* passion for Africa."

# CHAPTER 16

# The Nature of African Journeys

*I would rather live in a world where my life is surrounded by mystery than live in a world so small that my mind could comprehend it.*
—*Harry Emerson Fosdick*

My first visit to Africa brought me quickly to my knees. I was out of my element, out of my comfort zone, and it felt terrible. I'd lost my reference points and my sense of control. Time seemed to crawl, and in that strange, unfamiliar calm, I was bewildered by the intensity of my emotions and the depth of meaning in my experiences. Visits to rural Africa have that effect on people. These journeys are almost always uncomfortable, both physically and emotionally. They provide full immersion into a world completely different from the one we live in at home.

For most of us, our sense of reality and security is based entirely upon the things in our lives that are routine, comfortable, and familiar. Though there is nothing inherently wrong with these things, they can distract us from the need to have our reality and security come from God. Africa forces the issue. Those who journey to Africa are far away from home, and totally removed from the distractions of work and "doing." They are "disconnected" from the demands and hectic pace of their lives, and freed from e-mails, voice mails, faxes, and immediacy. In this strange new world, God seems more accessible. Yet I suspect we are the ones who have become more accessible to God.

I believe rural visits provide a unique "tent of meeting" for the Lord to speak to our individual and collective hearts. In the Bible, Moses sought out the presence of God when he:

> ". . . used to take the tent and pitch it outside the camp, a good distance from the camp and he called it the 'tent of meeting.' And it came about that everyone who sought the Lord would go out to the tent of meeting which was outside the camp."    Exodus 33:7

Seeing the beauty of God's creation is also an important part of the African experience. If nothing else, it allows us to see how big God is and how small we are.

Our trips to Africa are always physically demanding. Our itinerary is very aggressive, covering a number of countries in just a few days, often at breakneck speeds. We each take one carry-on backpack, and nothing more. We see some really tough situations and are collectively overcome with the enormity of the problems.

A few years ago, I was traveling with a group of entrepreneurs, most of whom were members of the Young Presidents Organization, an international group made up of people leading large corporations before the age of 40. It had been a long and arduous day filled with the requisite bumpy four-wheel-drive forays out of Kampala, Uganda, along Lake Victoria. We found ourselves in Masaka, Uganda. At that time, more than 30 percent of the population was infected with the HIV virus; that number is still growing. We spent the day traveling and working with World Vision staff, visiting their relief and educational efforts. It was a long, highly emotional day. We had been among the brokenhearted. It was hot. We were tired. We were ready for bed.

After a few more hours than we had bargained for, we finally rolled up in front of a ramshackle hotel that would serve as our shelter for the night. There were no lights, and in fact, the electricity for the entire village was not working. It seemed that nothing else in this hotel was working either. We were led through the dark and dingy halls by a shadowy figure whose face wasn't discernable behind the tattered, hooded robe he wore.

He carried a kerosene lantern, and two by two, we were shown our accommodations. It wasn't a pretty situation. With the power out, there was no running water, and toilets and sinks were backed up from previous use. The notion of housekeeping was a foreign one here. Out of the corner of my eye, I saw a mouse scamper into one of the rooms, and I shuddered to think what other critters might be lurking in the darkness.

The man with the lantern then made the rounds, and we gathered for a makeshift dinner. I ordered for the entire group: plain egg omelets cooked extra well done, accompanied by warm bottles of Stoney (an African version of our ginger ale). Hardly a word was spoken, and the setting was so grim, it seemed that our spirits might be dashed forever. This was a long and far cry from the five-star hotels these guys were accustomed to.

Exhausted, we paired up and ventured into our respective rooms for the night. As it turned out, none of us dared take off our clothes, let alone crawl under the well-worn and more-than-a-little scary covers on our beds.

The following morning brought renewed hope and energy. The sun was up, and we had survived the night. Our little group gathered on the severely leaning veranda of the dilapidated hotel, whose disrepair was even more evident in the full morning light. We disregarded the foul nature of our mugs, and enjoyed steaming coffee as we discussed our present situation.

"You're not going to believe what Bill said last night," exclaimed his roommate, Bob. "Whoa, hold on a minute," Bill quickly responded. "What we talked about last night was strictly between us. You can't violate roommate confidentiality!" Bob, with a wide smile on his face, said, "Oh, yes I can! We're all brothers here!" He went on to say that as they lay down on the grimy bedcovers and made makeshift pillows of their dirty clothes, Bill reached out to extinguish the glowing kerosene lantern, and looked over and said, "You know something? I'm WAY too rich to be in this place!"

We howled, and in fact, tears were streaming down our faces from laughing so hard. Nevertheless, what Bill said was true. We were in a place where we didn't feel comfortable. It wasn't nice. It wasn't clean. It wasn't critter-free. And it didn't feel particularly safe. But we were experiencing life like we'd never known it before. Once the laughter died down, we did some serious talking about the huge gap between the material comforts we take for granted and the basic human necessities that were provided here.

We realized this wasn't some high school field trip we were on—a one-time, just-passing-through deal. We were doing all we could to submerge ourselves in this totally new and different culture. Although we were feeling like aliens traveling through a time warp of hundreds of years of "progress," we recognized that this was the one-and-only, real world for the people living here. This was life. We were forced to ponder whose lifestyle most closely resembled reality. The most difficult part of the Africa experience is reconciling the contrasts between this world and our own, and incorporating the dramatic contrasts into a broader world view.

We agreed that we weren't here by accident. We were learning, albeit slowly. And that knowledge would necessarily force changes in our perspectives and our lives. God was becoming more real to us as we drew farther and farther away from the abundance and distractions of our lives back home. The trip gave us an opportunity to get a fleeting, but lasting glimpse of abject poverty, and we came away with a new and clear resolve to help communicate with others and hopefully become bridges to help span that gap. And, as I have discovered time and time again, the worst experiences often turn out to be the best ones. That grim night in the decrepit hotel, which certainly seemed to be the low point of the entire trip, in retrospect has proven to be one of the highlights.

Each day in Africa, we carve out time for prayer and devotions. It's a time when we, as a team, are able to "peel a few layers off the onion" as some of the emotional impact of the trip begins to wash over us. It's a simple fact that every traveler feels a bit overwhelmed (and perhaps even a little helpless) in trying to figure out how to connect the experiences of the trip with everyday life back home. It's always a challenging time, but also I believe it's the time when new doors are opened within us for God to step through.

As always, when the trip nears the end, the reality of the traveling group breaking up begins to sink in, as well as the larger question of what this trip will mean in each of our individual and collective lives.

Each time I come home, the question I get more than any other is, "How was your trip?"—often followed by either, "What did you do?" or "How did the team do?" As always, these questions are impossible to answer. Only time will tell. But whenever we return from Africa, there are always a handful of highly successful, Type A, controlling, businessmen wandering the downtown skyways of Minneapolis with eyes as big as dinner plates wondering, "What was that all about?"

The lessons, stories, laughs, and adventures that have come out of Africa would fill Lake Superior. While many believe that our going to Africa is to help or even "fix" the many problems in that part of the world, the reality is, it is *us* who get fixed! I think that for everyone who has ever gone on one of these journeys, there is a profound immediate effect as well as subsequent changes that take place later in their lives. These changes are the result of people allowing themselves to escape (however briefly) from the familiar and walk into new, unexplored regions of their own hearts and souls.

*Ward, Dave Durenberger, Steve Moore, and Mike Sime*

# Part Three

# Bridge Lessons

A follower of Jesus was camping in the mountains of Tibet. At sunset, two Sherpa herdsmen appeared out of the mist, and approached him at the campfire. They wore woolen robes, with hoods that partially obscured their dark, weathered faces. They said, "We have come a long way to get a word from you." After pondering for a moment how he might tell them about Jesus, the man of faith realized that these herdsmen would certainly understand sheep, so he began relating every Bible story he could remember that included shepherds and sheep. He recited Psalm 23, the lesson about the one lost sheep, Jesus as the Good Shepherd, and other sheep stories. When he finished, the herdsmen bowed deeply and retreated into the darkness. The following morning in the pre-dawn mist, the shepherds reappeared. They approached the man of faith and said, "We have discussed all through the night what you spoke about yesterday, and we have two very important messages in reply. The first is that we have decided to follow this God you call Jesus." Deeply moved, the man of faith then asked what the second message was. With eyes that danced with joy, the herdsmen said, "We have always known Him. We just didn't know His name!"

# Africa

# Introduction

*The significance of any event is dictated by its future.*
*—Monty Sholund*

*A pier is nothing other than a frustrated bridge. It is connected to one shore only and does not have another shore to attach itself to.*
*—Shimon Perez*

The groundwork for my first journey to Africa began in July of 1992 when I attended Stephen Covey's Principle Centered Leadership Conference in Sundance, Utah. I was intrigued with the concept of paradigms (how each of us views the world). Since our individual reality is filtered through a lifetime of personal experiences and observations, we have widely varying views of what comprises reality.

It wasn't difficult for me to conclude that my particular set of circumstances gave me a perspective on reality not widely shared by the majority of people in the world. So I decided to change my paradigm—intentionally. I believed that a trip to Africa—seeing poverty, suffering, and even death—would permanently affect the way I viewed my life and the world.

Little did I know . . .

I was a spiritual rookie traveling with a church group when I took my first trip to Africa. I had to insert little plastic tabs into my Bible just to locate the Scripture verses we were reading. And my comfort level with public prayer was low. The first time we formed a circle, held hands, and prayed together, the only prayer going through my head was "Please, God, don't let any of my clients or business associates see me here."

I was also quite taken aback at the airport when a group of "church ladies" approached us and started hugging us. They all wished me a good trip and told me that the Africa experience would change my life. I was disturbed by what they said. I had a wonderful life—and I didn't want it to change.

However, I soon discovered that, for better or worse, you can't change your paradigm without changing your life. From the moment I stepped onto African soil, my life was altered. At first, my whole being strained to take in the experiences, the people, the history, and the culture. Certain incidents were mind-boggling and heart-wrenching. The contrasts to my own life were extreme. It took months and years to make sense of it all, and to integrate the experiences into my life. My expanded world view continues to evolve.

From the time of my first trip, I have had one foot in America and one foot in Africa, and that duality of presence has grounded me in a whole new paradigm. In life and business and politics and faith, it was once easy to define myself in terms of what separated me from others. Africa has changed that. I now see myself as a bridge that spans two continents, and I look for common ground, believing there are no gaps too wide to be bridged. A Russian proverb inspires my way—*Go Godward: thou wilt find a road.*

The following stories illustrate some of the lessons I learned along the way.

# CHAPTER 17

# Finding the Hope in Hopelessness

*We can do no great things; only small things with great love.*
—*Mother Teresa*

*Where there is love, there is life.*
—*Mahatma Gandhi*

Though many people discount the transforming power of love, I have seen firsthand how it can make a difference. My third trip to Africa included an extra day in Nairobi, so we made plans to visit a World Vision-sponsored facility for orphaned children in Mathare Valley, one of the largest and most desperate slums on earth. As we left our relatively posh hotel and began winding our way through the streets of Nairobi, we were met by progressive levels of poverty. Just outside Mathare Valley, we stopped at a checkpoint and were then joined by two military guards, one carrying an M-16 automatic rifle and the other with an AK-47. From there, we entered an entirely different universe.

Mathare Valley, a section of Nairobi four kilometers long and two kilometers wide, serves as home to more than 400,000 people. It is a sprawling network of rubbish-strewn streets and running, open sewers, ramshackle shops, and homes fashioned out of every possible form of refuse—and it seems to stretch incessantly into a yawning mouth of endless despair. We were suddenly transported into a nightmare of Orwellian proportions, a garish quiltwork of bent, broken, and unpainted doom. We were in an endless maze of broken glass, old tires, barbed wire, and "keep out" signs. Scraggly dogs walked placidly by. Crudely fashioned kiosks displayed all manner of food and wares. Crates of chickens and produce of unknown origin were coated with dust and a greasy soot and petrol film from open fires and diesel fuel. Obscene smells hung over all with an unspoken profanity. The odors of cooking fires, garbage, diesel fumes, and waste were as oppressive and overbearing as the 95-degree temperature. The sun blazed unmercifully down upon dilapidated tin roofs secured over makeshift walls with rocks and bricks.

We took at least four left turns well past our comfort zone until we found ourselves at the tin-covered shanty which was serving as an orphanage for street children A sign announced the Kariobang Orphans Center. We stepped across open sewers, and entered a cement-floor "courtyard" which was about the size of the average kitchen in the U.S. There, 30 to 40 orphaned or abandoned children, infants to five-year-olds, were confined to a 15-by-20-foot classroom with a small, broken concrete play area, separated by a cracked wall from the slums beyond. These are among the most vulnerable children on the planet. It's been said that you  can gauge the well-being of a community by the abundance of smiles on the children's faces. But, despite our coaxing, the children didn't smile.

We were led inside a hot, cramped, covered area that served as the school's "shelter." On the floor was a filthy steel tub filled with unidentifiable beans and corn blended together in some type of porridge. The stew was covered with swarming flies. The air was thick with sweltering humidity and smoke from the cooking fire used to heat the stew. A small cup of this brew would be "lunch" for the children. For many, this would be their only meal of the day. We realized that what we were seeing was merely a microcosm of the millions of children in the shackles of abject poverty, without any love or affirmation. Our hearts cried out for some glimmer of hope for these kids. Poverty on this scale is much bigger than my ability to comprehend it—and seems like a massive crime in progress.

Two years later, I wanted to return to that same orphanage to allow others to witness the extreme despair and hopelessness I had seen. With the shock and traumatic emotions that I felt during my first visit in mind, I carefully and thoroughly explained the situation and provided an in-depth briefing on what we would be seeing.

You can imagine my surprise, delight, and bewilderment when we arrived at the orphanage and found that it had undergone an amazing transformation. We were greeted by smiling, singing children whose faces were beaming. They had formed a procession line and were jumping up and down with excitement. At first, I was convinced that we had come to the wrong address. The change was so dramatic. After a greeting from Rosemary Nuru, the orphanage director (the same woman who had hosted our previous visit), the children delivered a wonderful series of well-rehearsed and harmonized songs, which was followed by more laughter and celebration.

I quietly drew Rosemary aside and said, "I can't believe this is the same place we visited just two years ago. Can you tell me what happened? There is a night-and-day difference." She smiled, and shifted her gaze toward a small wooden bench along the dirty and cracked concrete wall that separated the orphanage from the street. Seated on the bench were three women who all appeared to be in their late 70s (although given the difficulty of lives here, it's very hard to accurately judge ages). My first impression was that they looked like three Mother Teresas in a row! Their heads were bowed, their hands folded, and they were either praying or asleep.

"Who are they? Where do they come from? What do they do?" I asked in typical American machine gun cadence. Rosemary explained that the women had come by the orphanage a year or so ago in search of work. Though she told them that she couldn't afford to pay them, they persisted, and said that they would work for free. Their job description was simple: to love the children. Every day since that time, the children have been greeted, nurtured, and loved by these three angels in disguise. She went on to say that the transformation was not immediate, but after just a few months of fostering, love, and attention, the results were much like pouring water on a dried-up garden.

The children had no more food than before. The orphanage building had progressively deteriorated since our last visit. The children's physical situation hadn't improved. Their clothes were still tattered and dirty. The specter of disease and hunger still clouded their futures. They had no books, no toys, no toothbrushes. The budget hadn't increased, and no new programs had been initiated.

The sole difference was the three women, and the only conclusion one could draw was that these children had become fully alive by the infusion of love and care into their lives. While I don't diminish the extreme challenges and difficulties these children face, I can no longer describe their situation as hopeless.

CHAPTER 18

# Mixing Church and State

*The answer to the question, "Am I my brother's keeper?" must always be, "No! I am my brother's brother."*    —Dr. Paul Klapper

I have always had an interest and fascination with politics. Up until my first trip to Africa, I was an ardent fundraiser and loved the political perks and pomp that came from being involved in national political races. In short, I was a political groupie. I wasn't passionate about issues or policy, but nevertheless loved dining with senators and congressmen, and being invited to exclusive parties and receptions.

As a result of my experiences in Africa, the surface relationships I'd had with a number of national political figures now had new dimension and higher purpose. These associations developed into true friendships. I came to realize that the vast majority of relationships these leaders have are conditional. Most of the people they deal with have agendas and want something. With that in mind, I decided to work on unconditional relationships based on friendship, quiet service, and prayer.

Over lunch one day in 1997, one of these political friends, Rod Grams, U.S. Senator from Minnesota, asked me if my invitation to travel to Africa was still open. I was stunned. In 1994, I had asked Rod to think about coming to Africa with me. He had rolled his eyes as he explained that his schedule as a Senator simply wouldn't accommodate a two-and-a-half week trip anywhere, let alone Africa. Now, three years later, without any prompting, he wanted to go. He went on to say that he wanted to go on the same type of trip I had been taking. It was not to be official business, and he didn't want to go in the role of a diplomat. He merely wanted to go as my friend and as someone interested in learning more about Africa. Plans were made, the itinerary was set, and in December 1997, we traveled to Africa.

Grams was then a member of the Foreign Relations Sub-Committee for Africa, and his going sparked more than a little interest, both in the U.S. and Africa. Since he was using personal vacation time, and it was not an official trip, we were able to circumvent normal complications imposed by the U.S. State Department. Protocol nevertheless demanded that the Senator meet with heads of state in the countries we visited. We met with Prime Minister Meles in Ethiopia, with President Museveni in Uganda, and with President Mkapa in Tanzania. Early on in those conversations, Rod always stressed that he hadn't come to Africa to teach or fix anything, but rather to learn. As a member of the Senate, he obviously had influence, but what he was looking for was perspective.

When he described the places deep in the bush we had visited in their countries, the presidents of those countries were amazed. "Why would you go there?" they would ask. "No one goes there." Grams would explain that we went to be with the people of the country and learn more about their traditions and cultures. He also explained that we were traveling together as a small group of friends, praying every day, reading Scripture together, and being open to God's leading. These were not typical diplomatic policy discussions. At the end of each meeting, Senator Grams provided all three presidents with his private direct-dial telephone number so they could stay in touch formally and as friends. I saw a tremendous potential for open communications and discussion based on friendship and knowledge.

The following year, in 1998, I accompanied former U.S. Senator David Durenberger to Africa. I had first met Dave during his successful Senate re-election bid in 1988. Given Dave's political involvement with Africa over the years, we had become friends. It turns out that Dave already had made a huge impact on Africa. In 1990, he had been asked to be the keynote speaker at an African Prayer Breakfast in Uganda, at which time he befriended President Museveni. He became an informed

influential advocate on behalf of many issues impacting the region. In doing so, he was also infected with the "disease of Africa." Africa was in his blood and in his heart. With even more diplomatic doors opened by the Grams trip, we were able to develop unconditional friendships with numerous other leaders in East Africa.

Right after Senator Grams agreed to go with me to Africa, I was in Washington, D.C., where I had the pleasure of meeting Doug Coe, a man of great faith who works quietly behind the scenes with members of the U.S. House and Senate. He asked me about my work in Africa, and I excitedly told him about the windpumps in West Pokot. Unlike many who have to feign interest in what has become a passion for me, Doug listened intently and with great interest. He encouraged me in all the work, and then very directly said, "Ward, if you were God, how would you help Africa?" I was a bit taken aback. As I later learned, Doug Coe's favorite strategy when encountering some-one for the first time is to throw a bean ball at his head! This was my bean ball.

I told him I didn't know how God would help Africa. "I understand," he said, "but let's just pretend. Would you build 1,000 windpumps?" "That would be great," I replied, picturing an army of windpumps across rural Africa. "Is that really the way you would do it?" he persisted. When he continued to press me, I replied that I would help the poor, the starving, the orphans, the least of the least, the poorest of the poor. "How?" he replied. "Well, I guess through people," I said. Off balance and feeling quite uncomfortable, I asked, "How do you think God would do it?" Coe replied, "I think He might start by changing the hearts of the leaders in Africa.

When I reflect on the visits that Rod and Dave and others have had with African leaders, I think that we have indeed provided encouragement and inspiration to them. I also think our willingness to listen to the burdens they carry—without retort or judgment—has been particularly appreciated. People in positions of power and authority are very often isolated from reality and lonely for real friends. Virtually every interaction of every day is conditioned upon at least some type of economic or political "quid pro quo." I think we have been able to genuinely demonstrate that our coming is not.

A couple of years ago, I had the honor of meeting Senator Jim Inhofe from Oklahoma. Up until that point, I knew him only by his reputation as a right wing conservative who wore cowboy boots with his business suit to the Senate floor. When we first met in his office, my prior image of him didn't fit the man I was speaking with. The first thing he did was pull out a copy of my book, *Life Through A Different Lens*, which chronicled the amazing experiences I had on my first trip to Africa in 1993. The book was tattered and frayed, and as he opened it, I saw that various sections were written in and highlighted. "Boy, Senator," I quipped, "You have an excellent staff to be able to have them pore over that book before I got here and make it look like you read it!" "No," Senator Inhofe replied, "I did read it. And you know what happened to you in this book? Well, the same thing happened to me."

In 1998, at the invitation of Doug Coe, Senator Inhofe traveled to Africa, not in a congressional delegation, but rather as an adventure in faith. Unlike formal Senatorial foreign relations trips, where the itinerary typically only includes airports, embassies, hotels, and state houses, Jim wandered far from the familiar to the "out-of-bounds" areas of Benin and Ghana. God spoke to his heart in a powerful way and set the hook for a deep calling to Africa. Senator Inhofe and his close friend, African Legislative Assistant, Mark Powers, have traveled twice a year to Africa ever since.

They have visited Benin, Nigeria, Burkina Fasso, Togo, Ghana, Cote d'Ivoire, Niger, Gabon, Democratic Republic of the Congo, Burundi, Kenya, Rwanda, and Uganda, with brief stops in Jijibouti, Tunisia, and Senegal. This extraordinary level of commitment to Africa underscores a correspondingly extraordinary calling. In his role as a key U.S. Senator, Jim has an open door to the presidents of every country he visits. Yet, when he visits them, he comes not as a senator, but rather as a friend and a brother.

Back in Washington, Senator Inhofe hosts a luncheon the third Thursday of each month for the African ambassadors of the countries he's befriended. This has created friendships and relationships that go well beyond the normal diplomacy dictated by protocol. As a U.S. Senator, Inhofe's time is his most elusive asset. Yet, Jim gives it away freely when friends come from Africa, and he is constantly connecting these friends in very important, if unspoken ways. He has become an amazing ambassador, not only for his country, but also for Jesus, with the simple message of love and reconciliation. His office has literally become a "light on the hill."

Senator Inhofe, along with many other leaders in the United States, Africa, and the world, are becoming the bridges that connect our dissimilar worlds. Their foundations are friendships and relationships built around prayer and the reconciling principles of Jesus. These human bridges are providing in-creased understanding, candid dialogue, and the mutual respect that underscores friendship. It is my experience that bridges get walked upon—sometimes in good faith, sometimes in malice. But by being connectors of people and ideas, they can go a long way in helping to provide mutual understanding and encourage-ment among people from very different cultures and paradigms.

# CHAPTER 19

# Fraternizing with the Enemy

*In the practice of tolerance, one's enemy is the best teacher.*
— *Fourteenth Dalai Lama*

*It is easy enough to be friendly to one's friends. But to befriend the one who regards himself as your enemy is the quintessence of true religion. The other is mere business.* —*Mahatma Gandhi*

Haven't we met before?" asked the man seated next to me at the table. I replied somewhat curtly that we had not. He extended his hand, so we shook hands and introduced ourselves. I already knew who he was, and took a deep breath, realizing that it might be difficult for me to remain civil to him. I considered him an enemy, and was braced for a confrontation. We were at an executive luncheon sponsored by Church Metro, and he was going to be the featured speaker. This man, Tim McGuire, was editor of the *Minneapolis Star Tribune*, a newspaper that, in my opinion, had become a left wing, liberal platform for virtually everything I considered wrong with our political system.

Tim indicated he knew my name from somewhere, and I then told him that I had written numerous letters to him in his capacity as editor of the *Star Tribune*. A look of realization crossed his face, and he said, "That's it! Now I remember." This was followed by a fairly uncomfortable pause, and I figured that would be the end of our conversation.

Then someone at the table who was aware of my frequent travels to East Africa asked about my plans for the next trip, which was coming up in two months. Tim turned to me and said, "I had one of my most powerful spiritual experiences in South Africa." He went on to say that he had traveled to South Africa in January of 1993 as part of a national group of newspaper editors at the invitation of Nelson Mandela, who had recently been released from prison. Although the interaction with Mandela and the high-profile activities were interesting, the most powerful imprint on his heart was a church service he attended in a desperately poor section of Soweto. He went on to describe a nearly three-hour church service. It struck me that I had been through an almost identical experience in the same place, only three months apart from his. It was in 1994 during the months immediately preceding the national elections. The world was predicting (with good cause) a blood bath. As it turned out, Tim and I had both been given an opportunity to experience the same tensions, anxieties, and tears of a congregation of believers locked in fervent prayer.

As he was describing his experience, which was eerily and surprisingly close to my own, a funny thing happened. I started to pray for him. Somehow I was able to break through the protective shell of economic, social, and political differences. I was able to break through the stored up animosity and resentment after I had caught a glimpse of his heart.

As he walked up to the lectern to deliver his address, I continued to pray. I was amazed by what I heard. It seemed a "coming out" of sorts, as he proclaimed Jesus as his friend and savior. When he inevitably touched on social or economic issues, I was able to acknowledge the difference of opinion, but it never altered my ability to hear what his heart was saying. It was an amazing experience for me to see this man, who has such a prominent position in the community, openly and honestly sharing his own shortcomings as well as the importance of Jesus in his life.

Perhaps the biggest surprise came when I encountered a close friend who had been sitting just a few tables away. On our way out, I made the comment, "Wasn't that an amazing talk?" He responded, "Yeah. Can you believe the hypocrisy of that man!" I was dumbfounded. My friend went on to enumerate instance after instance where he thought McGuire had allowed his liberal perspective to dominate the message. I was amazed! Had he heard the same talk? Had he even been in the same room? How could our impressions have been so far apart?

It was only after this convicting encounter that I realized the far-reaching impact of that single (albeit powerful) spiritual experience in the slums of South Africa. I was finally able to see in my "enemy" the person deep beneath the facade of stark political differences. I had prayed for him, and I believe that prayer allowed God to remove the barriers of entrenched doctrines and differences so that I could capture what his heart was trying to say. It was a moment of tremendous grace.

It has been said that it is impossible to hate someone for whom you are praying. I now see the truth in that. Having said that, the questions remain, "Did he win you over politically? Did you win him over?" The answer in both cases is "no." I suspect that we remain diametrically opposed on most every aspect of public and social policy. He's liberal, and I'm conservative. But I no longer think of him as ill-intentioned or dumb. He is light years from either. I do believe we have vastly different perspectives on how to transform our society and the world, but our objectives are the same. As he put it in his talk, we need "to see Jesus' face in everyone we meet."

I saw Jesus in Tim McGuire's life, and I am now proud to be able to call him my friend.

The luncheon was a painful but important opportunity to examine how my own experiences and resulting prejudices put me at odds with the command to "love your enemies." It also caused me to grapple with the question, "Who is my brother?" It's easy to criticize hatred in others, yet difficult to see and understand the darkness in ourselves. Situations like this beg the question of whether we are capable of truly loving our enemies while remaining steadfast in our own preferred means to uphold our values and principles.

Abraham Lincoln once commented to a woman who couldn't believe he was fraternizing with an arch political rival, "Madam, do I not destroy enemies by making them my friends?"

I think he was on to something . . .

# Chapter 20

# Relations vs. Relationships

*The opportunity to practice brotherhood presents itself every time you meet a human being.* —*Jane Wyman*

*Do not wait for leaders; do it alone, person to person.* —*Mother Teresa of Calcutta*

Back in 1993, the United States was embroiled in the unfolding tragedy in Somalia, a country in the horn of East Africa. Through media reports, the world learned of the famine and starvation there. Initially, the U.S. launched Operation Restore Hope, which provided peacekeeping troops and food relief to the country. Unfortunately, the vast majority of the donated food was hijacked by Somali warlord factions, further disrupting Somalia's suffocating agricultural markets. In an effort to restore order, U.S. military forces invaded Mogadishu. As the conflict escalated, U.S. soldiers were captured and 19 were killed. Corpses of American soldiers were dragged through the muddy streets of Mogadishu by cheering Somali soldiers. The event was horrifically played out on television broadcasts to the American people. What had begun as a humane gesture by the United States had resulted in a diplomatic and logistical nightmare.

Pressure grew steadily on the Clinton administration to clarify its reasons for keeping large numbers of American troops in Somalia without clear purpose and an end in sight. The original intent was to bring an end to the fighting by capturing the Somali warlord General Mohammed Farah Aideed. From late summer into the fall, the U.S. military had searched for Aideed without success, while the pressure at home for U.S. withdrawal kept building.

In mid-October the President asked all members of Congress to meet in the Capitol with Secretary of State Warren Christopher and Secretary of Defense Les Aspin. Though Christopher and Aspin said they were there to get advice regarding what course of action the U.S. should follow, members of the House and Senate were irate over the situation, and tempers flared. The meeting ended abruptly.

During this same time period, two African heads of state were visiting in Washington, D.C. Their visits were not formally recognized by the U.S. State Department, and no official meetings had been arranged. This seemed to underscore the indifference of the U.S. towards Africa.

The morning after the heated and unsuccessful Congressional meeting, Dave Durenberger attended the weekly Senate Prayer Breakfast in the Capitol. There he met the two visiting African leaders, President Isaias Afwerke of Eritrea and President Melchior Ndadaye of Burundi. Dave stayed after the meeting for a cup of coffee and some informal conversation. He was astounded when President Afwerke said, "Everybody in East Africa loves the United States and wants to see you successful in whatever endeavor you engage. But we are mystified by your presence in Somalia. How is it that the most high-tech country in the world can't find one man in a no-tech country?" Then Afwerke pulled a piece of paper out of his pocket, wrote briefly on it, and handed it to Dave, saying, "If you want to find Aideed, try him at this telephone number." The number was Aideed's personal line at the Serena Hotel in Nairobi.

While all of this was taking place, I was in Nairobi on my second trip to East Africa. I was, in fact, staying at the Serena Hotel. One morning after breakfast, I was returning to my room on the fifth floor. I hit the "up" button, and mindlessly got off when the elevator stopped. As I walked down the hall, I noticed all the doors were open, and each room seemed to contain two or three men whose height and apparent strength could have qualified them for the National Basketball Association. Before I knew it, four or five of these towering men surrounded me, and I realized I was in deep trouble. "So this is how it happens when you get robbed in Nairobi," I thought. One of the men asked me, "Where are you going?" I replied with a quavering voice, "I'm just going to my room." "Show me your key," he demanded. It was then that I realized what the routine must be. They get your room key, take you to your room, kill you, rob you, and then flee.

As I removed the key to room 504 from my pocket and showed it to him, he simply pointed to the elevator, which indicated we were on the sixth floor. "Wrong floor," he said. I was flooded with relief. The men escorted me back to the elevator with solemn nods and saw me off.

I immediately went to the check-in desk and asked the receptionist what was going on up on the sixth floor. She averted her eyes and said, "We are not allowed to say anything about that." I was still confused, but nevertheless relieved.

Later that morning, I was entering the elevator in the lobby of the Serena. As the doors opened, I collided with a small, wiry man holding an ornate walking stick, and nearly knocked him down. As I grabbed his arm and looked into his eyes, I realized with a shock that I was holding the arm of Mohammed Aideed, the very same warlord the CIA had publicly been seeking to capture, dead or alive. I recognized him vaguely from the photographs that I'd seen, but most distinctly by the walking stick that had become his trademark. No words were exchanged, but our eyes did lock. I was filled with an undefined fear and foreboding. Aideed was accompanied by two of my tall new friends from the sixth floor, and just a few minutes later, I saw them sipping iced tea in a cabana by the pool.

Back to Washington, D.C., and the conversation with Senator Durenberger and the African heads of state. "Aideed and his troops will never surrender, and this is a war you can't possibly win, short of destroying the entire country, unless you seek a new way forward," said President Afwerke. "So what would you suggest as this new way forward?" Dave asked. "I would start by talking with Aideed and expressing an interest in building a new and better relationship," President Afwerke replied. When Dave asked if these opinions had been shared with anyone from the State Department or the Clinton administration, the answer was, "No."

Needless to say, Dave didn't wait long to pick up the phone, call the White House, and ask for his friend David Gergen, who was then the special assistant to President Clinton. Dave commiserated with Gergen about the unfortunate meeting with Christopher and Aspin the previous afternoon. Then Dave asked Gergen if he would like to establish contact with the elusive Aideed. The astonished Gergen replied, "You've got to be kidding!" Dave gave him the number. Gergen, still disbelieving, said, "You're saying if I call this phone number, Aideed will answer?" Dave replied, "I got the number from President Afwerke. They are friends . . ." Later Gergen was able to use that number to begin a dialogue that resulted in a new relationship and, ultimately, a phased withdrawal of U.S. troops.

Certainly diplomacy and foreign relations are critical to establishing world order and peace, and protocol and legalism are necessary components of this vital form of communication. Nevertheless, an important underpinning for relationships among leaders of different countries can be the candor, trust, and accountability that come with personal relationships and friendships.

Another example of effective personal relationships that lead to effective diplomatic relations is this story related by Doug Coe. In 1980, he took a trip to East Africa with his youngest son, Jonathan. The purpose of the trip was to meet with various leaders, with whom Doug had formed relationships over the years. But equally important, the trip was to demonstrate to his son, Jonathan, how effective the message of Jesus can be outside of America and the constraints of organized religion.

They were at the airport in Mogadishu, the capital of Somalia, for a three-hour refueling stop. Doug was surprised when a man he had never met came up to him and asked if he was Doug Coe. Doug responded, "Yes," and was led with Jonathan to a car at the edge of the tarmac. Without any further conversation, they were driven through the narrow, winding streets of Mogadishu. They finally arrived at a nondescript residence.

They were led up a flight of stairs where a Muslim man Doug did not know greeted them. After welcoming them to his home, the man wanted to know something about Doug and his son, Jonathan, as well as what they were doing there. A bit off balance, but ever game for a new relationship, Doug explained his passion for working with leaders in Africa and throughout the world to discuss the precepts and principles of Jesus of Nazareth with them. He went on to explain that he felt called to free the message of Jesus from the box of organized and denominational Christianity. They talked, and shared, and laughed together. As the time drew close for them to leave for the airport, Doug, now much more comfortable with this "new friend," reached over and asked if they could pray together. "That would be wonderful," the host replied.

As they rose to leave, the man took Doug by the arm and asked, "What will you be doing in Nairobi?" "We're going to spend some time with President Moi," Doug responded.

"Would you be so kind as to give him a message from me?" the man asked. "I would like him to know that if we were able to get together this way and pray together, I think we could solve the problem of the current border dispute between Kenya and Somalia."

Doug's eyebrows went up, and he said, "I'd be happy to deliver that message, but I'm not exactly sure who to tell him that it's from."

"I am Siad Barre, the President of Somalia," the man replied.

CHAPTER 21

# Fixing Broken Hearts

*We often hear it said, "If God existed there would be no wars." But it would be truer to say: If God's laws were observed there would be no wars.*                                    —Yves M. Congar

*We must be at war with evil, but at peace with men.*
                                        —J.E.E. Dalberg-Action

I was filled with a sense of dread. I was on a small plane with Senator Durenberger, headed for Rwanda. The State Department was against our going. The risks were great. We were flying into a country that in 1994 saw more than 800,000 of its citizens murdered by their neighbors in one of the most horrific cases of genocide in world history. As the pilot announced that we had crossed over the Tanzanian border into Rwanda, I was struck by the beautiful and serene landscape below. I also was filled with a profound, inexplicable foreboding that quickly turned into sorrow. As we flew over an increasingly beautiful landscape that many call the "Switzerland of Africa," I was overcome by a deep sense of anguish, almost immediately followed by an equally deep sense of rebuke. Why was I now close to tears as I considered the tragedy that had occurred in this country in 1994? I had already been to Africa five times, so why was it only now (four years after the fact) that the reality of the horror was hitting home? Why now and not then? Was it only through a personal visit that I could be overwhelmed by the dreadfulness of such recent history?

We stayed at the Hotel des Milles Collines, which had been a safe haven provided by the hotel's manager for many of the Tutsis during the genocide. We had an appointment to see an old friend, Charles Murigande, who was then Secretary General of Rwanda's ruling party, and a close friend and advisor to Rwanda President, Paul Kagame. Murigande had received his Ph.D. and was teaching at Howard University in Washington, D.C. when news of the genocide first reached the U.S. Upon hearing about the genocide, Charles immediately resigned his teaching position and informed his department head that he was returning to Rwanda. "You can't go, Charles. You will be killed! Hundreds and thousands of people are being slaughtered." Then, as an aside, he said, "Besides, you can't just  leave your job. I need time to get a replacement to teach your classes." Charles replied in his lilting French-laced accent, "You will fill my position in three weeks. My country will never be able to fill my position." Despite the tremendous risk and danger, Charles returned to join General Paul Kagame as a leader in the Rwandan Patriotic Front (RPF) that finally restored stability and civility to Rwanda.

As Dave and I were waiting in the hotel lobby, we noticed a small group of Rwandans in a corner reading the Bible together. We introduced ourselves, and the Senator explained that many of his colleagues in the House and Senate had been praying for Rwanda. Now that he was here, he wondered if there were specific things for which they would have us pray. The leader replied in French, and through the beautiful, buoyant accent of the interpreter, he informed us with sad and somber eyes that we should pray for three things: (1) stability in Rwanda, (2) continued healing and reconciliation among the Hutus and Tutsis, and, most importantly, (3) the brokenhearted. We prayed together, and neither Dave nor I could speak as we left.

Later that evening, we went to the Murigande home, and met with Charles, his lovely wife Rosette, and other friends in various positions of leadership within the government. They had been praying together as a group every Wednesday evening since the genocide began in 1994.

The encounter with the study group in the hotel lobby was still fresh in our minds, so we asked the assembled group of friends, "How do you pray for a broken heart?" I was moved by the responses. First of all, we were told that in praying for the broken hearted, we need to recognize that it includes not only the victims (the many widows, widowers, and orphans from the genocide), but also the perpetrators who had participated in the mass killings. With that in mind, he went on to say, "It's impossible to fix a broken heart. What you need to pray for is that those with broken hearts might find new ones."

Sitting with Charles and our new friends in Rwanda, I heard first-hand stories of horror and heartbreak that I could absorb mentally, but had a hard time comprehending at the heart level. The idea of neighbors and friends attacking each other with machetes, and hacking and being hacked to death, was chilling. One person related a story of a small girls' school that was confronted by a group of Hutu soldiers. The soldiers ordered the girls to divide themselves up into lines, with Hutus in one and Tutsis in the other. The girls refused, because they saw themselves neither as Hutus or Tutsis, but as friends. These children were not yet indoctrinated in tribal prejudice and racism. As a result, they were massacred together in a startling demonstration of loyalty and courage.

We heard story after story of broken hearts. Henriette Sebera related how, when the genocide began in 1994, she and some other women fled with their babies from their rural village in southeastern Rwanda to the bush. The women intentionally split up from their husbands and went in opposite directions so that in the event the Interahamwe killers found one of them, their children wouldn't be totally orphaned. During previous times of sporadic genocide, the Christian Church had always been a safe place, so the women left their babies in a church during the day and snuck back to feed and care for them at night.

On the third day, near daybreak, Henriette's husband didn't show up for their scheduled rendezvous. She knew in her heart that he had been killed. Henriette was overcome with grief as she stoically returned to the church alone to feed her babies. When she opened the door, she was horrified to see her babies, and all the other babies, dead and butchered on the altar.

Everyone had a story. Agnes Mukabaranga, now a lawyer and prominent member of the Rwandan General Assembly, told of the terror of having to hide with her family at a Congolese neighbor's home considered "safe" from the Hutu killing rampage. When the neighbors evacuated the area after two weeks, Agnes and her family returned to their own home, where they hid under the beds and in the trees in the garden. With the help of a guard, ten children escaped to Burundi under a  mattress in the back of a pickup truck. Agnes and the other adults remained at her home, always hidden, wasting away from lack of food, and unendingly frightened by the noise of bullets and bombs. They survived because the soldiers, who had entered the house many times, did not find the room where they were hiding. Every day for three months they lived in dread of being discovered and summarily butchered.

Unlike the terrorist attack on America or other singular disasters whose lifespan can be measured in hours or days, Rwanda's nightmare continued unabated for three entire months. Throughout those months people awoke to a living nightmare of screams, terror, and murder. The rivers flowing through the country carried an unrelenting, macabre procession of mutilated corpses. For Agnes, Henriette, and every Rwandan who survived, the greatest question during this ordeal must have been, "Where is the rest of the world? Is anyone coming to help us?"

Those who survived the genocide now have the burden of their memories as well as the challenge of sharing with the world their stories of a time and place where evil ran rampant. Stories of young children brutally killed in front of their parents, with often one parent spared so that he or she would have to endure a lifetime of tortuous memories. Stories of women raped and mutilated in front of the disbelieving eyes of husbands, families, and friends who themselves would soon be victims. Stories of Tutsi households attacked in the middle of the night, and bodies of family members (some dead, some alive) unceremoniously dumped into open-pit latrines. Stories of domesticated dogs, whose owners had died, turning wild and roaming the countryside devouring human bodies. Stories of hell on earth.

Over a span of three months, more than 800,000 Rwandans were savagely murdered in a geographic area the size of Massachusetts. One-tenth of the total population of Rwanda was annihilated. In terms of human loss, the genocide in Rwanda was equivalent to 200 World Trade Centers.

With these stories and facts fresh in our minds, we visited the genocide memorial. Throughout Rwanda, there are specified sites where the bodies of those massacred are left in full ghastly repose in the precise location where they were slain. There is nothing left now but bloody, tattered clothing covering dry bones. We were taken to a newly constructed memorial site in Kigali, Rwanda, where the bodies of more than 200,000 victims were buried. We went to a room where there were literally hundreds and hundreds of broken skulls on a table. Charles Murigande turned to me and asked, "Ward, can you tell me which ones were Hutus and which were Tutsis?" As I looked at the skulls, they all seemed similar. I turned to Charles with questioning eyes. He stated, "You can't, and that's the real tragedy."

In a meeting the following morning, Paul Kagame, the newly instituted President of Rwanda, explained to us the tremendous challenges that face his country. In total, more than a million people were killed in the genocide. One hundred percent of the remaining people were displaced from their homes. Imagine that! *Every* person was, at least for a period of time, a refugee. The country was bankrupted, and the entire infrastructure destroyed. As Kagame pointed out, if a natural disaster, disease, or famine had struck Rwanda, the world would have come rushing in with an outpouring of love, care, and aid. Not so with genocide. The world that shunned Rwanda and refused to offer assistance before and during the genocide was now just as reluctant to help rebuild a country so crippled emotionally, structurally, and politically.

The world is usually critical of human rights injustices, and attention has turned to the tens of thousands who were locked up in Rwandan jails and charged with murder following the genocide. Kagame asked, "Is your American justice system equipped to handle more than 100,000 capital murder cases simultaneously?" He explained that the only workable form of justice was to have three witnesses collaborate the guilt of a perpetrator, which was sufficient for imprisonment. Obviously, there are at least some innocent people in jail. What should be done? Releasing the prisoners would be a clear invitation for genocide to continue among the perpetrators as well as those seeking justice and/or revenge. Though the world would like to levy a "quick fix," this is a problem that clearly demands thoughtful consideration and a deep sense of understanding. As Kagame said, "Although we are interested in the opinions of our critics, they are the same critics who stood by during the genocide and did nothing to stop it."

I am happy to report that in the years since my first visit, Rwanda has become a place of healing. In 2002, Federal Judge Paul Magnuson traveled with me to Rwanda. He was there as part of a State Department delegation representing the International Judicial Relations Committee, which offers developing countries the models and precepts of America's judicial system.

In Rwanda, nearly one million people lost their lives in 100 days. As a result of the genocide, about 120,000 people were placed in pre-trial detention. The Arusha accords led to the establishment of an international tribunal to hear war crimes against the alleged perpetrators of the Rwandan genocide. In eight years, ten defendants have been tried. With the impossible overflow of pending genocide-related criminal cases within the Rwandan judicial system, it was decided that charges stemming from the genocide would be settled by the traditional, time-honored system of village justice called Gacaca Courts (literally meaning "justice on the grass"). In essence, the village chief and elders are responsible for listening to both the alleged perpetrators and the surviving victims to determine innocence or guilt, as well as the nature and severity of the punishment.

Judge Magnuson met with acting Gacaca judge Jean-Pierre, who speaks primarily French. Jean-Pierre related that his mother, his sister, and his lawyer had been killed, but he didn't know who had killed them. Jean-Pierre told of returning to his home village to demonstrate how Gacaca Courts would work. In setting up an example, he selected a detainee at random. He asked the person if he would confess. The detainee said, "Yes." He asked if the detainee had killed anyone. The detainee said, "Yes." He asked whom the detainee had killed. "I killed your mother. I killed your sister. I killed your lawyer."

"How could you possibly have listened to this confession from the man who had killed your own family?" asked Judge Magnuson.

"I had no other choice," said Jean-Pierre. "I have seen the devastating effects of revenge in our country, and it has to stop someplace. Otherwise, the killing goes on, and on, and on. I chose to have it stop with me. I forgave him. We must be reconciled, one to another."

CHAPTER 22

# Salt and Light

*It is for us to see the Kingdom of God as always coming, always pressing in on the present, always big with possibility, and always inviting immediate action.* —*Walter Rauschenbusch*

*Blessed are the peacemakers, for they will be called sons of God.*
—*Jesus*

When I met Samuel Nimubona, he greeted me with a smile that seemed to spread literally from ear to ear . . . and it was contagious. To know Samuel was to love him. He had a deep passion for the problems of his homeland and an even greater faith in God's ability to solve them.

Samuel and his closest friend, leading businessman Prosper Turimuci, have been powerful change instruments in Burundi, a tiny, yet beautiful country, barely distinguishable on a map of Africa. Located between its giant neighbors, The Democratic Republic of the Congo and Tanzania, Burundi shares its northern border with Rwanda. The country has survived many trials and tribulations including deep ethnic divisions and sporadic genocide between its two leading tribes, the Hutus and the Tutsis. In 1993, Burundi's first democratically elected president was assassinated, and tremendous instability followed.

At the time of my first visit there in 1999—with Senator Durenberger, Eric Fellman, Tekle Selassie, Sam Owen, my son Andy, and my sister Heidi—we found Burundi to be a deeply divided country, isolated from the rest of the world by the recently lifted embargo. Economic ruin, poverty, devastation, and instability had created a playground for the devil. But it also was a wonderful place, and an opportunity for God to show His hand.

God showed His hand through Samuel, Prosper, and Burundi Cabinet Minister Bernard Barandereka. Encouraged by the small groups that were meeting and praying within business and political circles both in Washington, D.C., and surrounding countries in Africa, Samuel, Prosper, and Bernard decided to start such a group in Bujumbura, Burundi's capital city. They reached out to all sides of leadership, despite seemingly insurmountable political and tribal differences. They made it clear that all participants were to temporarily put aside partisan politics and issues, and simply meet together to pray and share their lives.

Augustin Nzojibwami, leader of the Hutu opposition in the Burundi National Assembly, had declined to be part of the new small group that was now meeting weekly. But Samuel refused to give up on him. So, when Samuel learned about a gathering in South Africa of small groups from various countries that would be meeting to pray, fellowship, and discuss the problems of Africa, he invited Augustin to attend. Samuel also invited Augustin's political opponent and apparent "enemy," Prosper Turimuci.

Unbeknownst to either of them, Samuel arranged for them to be seated next to each other on the flight to Johannesburg. After a cordial pre-takeoff conversation, Augustin turned to Prosper and asked his name. "I am Prosper Turimuci," he replied. At that, Augustin left his seat with a terrified expression on his face.

Quickly realizing there was nowhere else to go, Augustin reluctantly returned and said, "You cannot be Prosper Turimuci. He is a bad man. A killer! Have you been sent to kill me?" "No," replied Prosper. "I have never killed anyone. I am a businessman, and a family man. I only want the killing and violence to stop!"

Augustin went on to say that Prosper had been deemed by Hutu factions to be one of their greatest enemies. Augustin had heard—and believed—terrible rumors about Prosper. But now, face to face, as they shared stories of family and a common dream for peace in Burundi, they became fast friends. Upon their return to Burundi, Augustin bravely went on the airwaves to discuss this newfound relationship with someone who had been purported to be his enemy. Having shared their lives together for just a few days, they were able to see how distorted their prior viewpoints were from reality. Disagreements remained on method, but they found common ground on purpose and dream. They both had families they dearly loved. They shared the same love for Burundi. They shared the same God.

A miracle had begun, and reconciliation was taking place. These two "new" brothers began appealing to their respective leaders, both Hutu and Tutsi, to come together in fellowship and prayer to talk candidly about the things that divided them and the things that united them. They jointly issued a call to end the demonizing of each other's positions.

Word of the small prayer group spread, and their numbers grew. In 2002, the group decided to demonstrate its new spirit of national unity and held the first Burundi National Prayer Breakfast in Bujumbura. Nearly all of the government and business leaders attended, including President Pierre Buyoya and his wife, Sofie.

I will never forget the close of that "breakfast" meeting—at 4:30 p.m.! At the invitation of the host committee, a renowned Hutu opposition leader addressed the delegation as follows: "I didn't want to come to this breakfast when Samuel and Augustin invited me. But when I learned it would be centered on the principles and precepts of Jesus, I felt an obligation to attend, because I am a follower. I had intended to make only a brief appearance. Instead, I have been here all day, and I have been deeply moved by the many stories, testimonies, and prayers given by those I had regarded as my enemies. But this moment is most amazing. To have been invited up to the front of this assembly to give the closing prayer represents a miracle of reconciliation and a new way forward."

Quietly behind it all was the ever-smiling Samuel, bringing people together in prayer and friendship before discussing issues and differences.

Although a cease-fire agreement was signed in Arusha in 2002, one major rebel force, the FNL, remains outside the cease-fire treaty, and the violence continues. The transitional government is made up of both Hutu and Tutsi leaders with periodic transfers of power planned over the next few years. Samuel helped orchestrate meetings with Parliamentary leaders in Tanzania, which greatly enhanced relations between these neighboring countries, and have opened the way for dialogues with the rebel groups outside of the peace negotiations.

It is a tragedy that when peace comes to Burundi, and I hope in my heart it will soon, Samuel, God's soft and gentle peacemaker, will not be there. He operated in the demarcation zones where reconciliation was only a dream, agendas often clashed, and his work was sometimes perceived as a threat. On September 7, 2002, in a residential area of Bujumbura, Samuel was assassinated. Initial reports stated that Samuel was not the intended victim, and that he had been caught in crossfire and accidentally killed. Later it was determined that Samuel had taken seven bullets to the head. Ultimately, he lost his life to the same senseless conflict and violence he had devoted his life to preventing. He is survived by his wife, Delphine, and their two young daughters. He was 33 years old.

However, even in death, Samuel continues to bring Burundi together. An outdoor memorial service for him was attended by more than a thousand friends and leaders from every ethnic background, political party, religion, and denomination within Burundi. These people came to mourn the loss of Samuel, and yet to celebrate their wonderful friend, Burundi's ambassador for peace, who connected people, places, and hearts. Through him, they saw God move mountains.

# CHAPTER 23

# Sharing the Pain

*Benevolence doesn't consist in those who are prosperous pitying and helping those who are not. Benevolence consists in fellow feeling that puts you upon actually the same level with the fellow who suffers.* —*Woodrow Wilson*

There is a very dangerous tendency in America to glamorize the poor in the developing nations of the world. During our frequent journeys to Africa, we often are in areas of abject poverty, where people are seemingly miserable and stuck without hope. We, on the other hand, are just passing through.

It's far too easy for those experiences to resemble the snapshots we take with our cameras—freeze-framed images that are collected throughout a breakneck itinerary. When attempting to share our experiences with friends and family at home, we have to categorize and catalogue them in order to make any type of coherent presentation. We hope our stories about the poorest of the poor will be interesting and hopefully heartrending. Pictures of emaciated children, stooped women, and crippled men bring reactions of disbelief and compassion from those who view them. Often the response we get is almost congratulatory in nature (or perhaps even feelings of pity for *us*) for having witnessed, first-hand, humanity in misery.

There is nothing noble about witnessing suffering.

These situations *are not* freeze-framed photos or journalistic replays. They involve very real people who are living in situations often wildly beyond our comprehension. Although as visitors we share some brief moments, prayers, and emotional good-byes, we are soon on our way to the next stop, the next destination, the next set of images before ultimately winging our way back across the Atlantic to lives both familiar and comfortable. But the desperate lives and tragic circumstances we leave in Africa grind on in real time long after our psychological photo albums are put away.

Situations almost too cruel to ponder are still being played out—as I sit in the serenity and comfort of my study. Tears are being shed, mothers are being buried, children are being raised without love or hope. People's lives, full of unimaginable challenges and hardships beyond description, are going forward in the very places we stood. The only change is our lack of presence. There is a universe of difference between observed pain and shared pain. These nightmares and tragedies don't disappear just because we do.

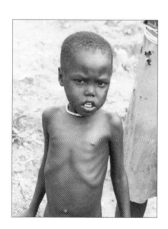 

CHAPTER 24

# Faith Squared

*It is neither necessary nor indeed possible, to understand any matter of faith farther than it is revealed.* —*Benjamin Whichcote*

I met Kurkura Wafo when he was World Vision Director in the Antsokia Valley, located in a remote section of north central Ethiopia.

Kurkura had led the life of a slave during his upbringing by distant relatives in a remote Muslim village and was banished from his family and community when they discovered that he had secretly decided to follow Jesus as the result of a chance encounter at Missionary School.

Forced to live on his own from childhood, Kurkura was subsequently jailed during the Communist regime and suffered unimaginable torture simply for his refusing to renounce Jesus as his Lord. As he described the whippings, electric prods, and relentless beatings within the wretched confines of the dark prison in Addis Ababa, I could only imagine my own reaction, which would probably have been: "Lord, I need to renounce you for these guys, so that they won't kill me. That way, I'll be able to do a lot of good later on."

But it was during Kurkura's recent visit to Minneapolis that I realized, once again, the many mysteries of faith, and how inscrutable they can be.

After spending a day together, I was taking Kurkura to the airport, and I asked him if there were things I could pray about for him and his family. He replied that there were three areas needing prayer. His first request was that I pray that he might have more time with his family. Working at a World Vision project in southern Ethiopia, he was only able to return to his home in Addis Ababa once a month, for three to four days. He was really sorry not to be able to see his children growing up. His second prayer request was that his children might be able to attend a better school. In Ethiopia, all good standard schools are private, requiring tuition. Given his annual salary of about $6,000 per year, he could not afford the better schools for his children. The third concern had to do with his job. Silently, I immediately starting thinking about my connections to the World Vision organization, and about the strings and levers I could pull regarding any problems Kurkura was having.

Kurkura went on to say, "The problem is that I have been asked to be a department head for Christian Witness within the World Vision office in Addis Ababa."

I looked at him in disbelief, and with my arm raised for a high five, I said, "Congratulations, Kurkura!"

I figured that he had been putting me on about the three areas of concern, because obviously this newest development clearly answered those prayers. Kurkura didn't smile, and softly he told me that when he learned of this opportunity, both he and his wife went to the Lord in prayer.

"God said, 'No,'" Kurkura replied.

I was shocked. I know myself well enough to know that if I had similar prayer requests, I would have assumed that the job promotion was in answer to those prayers.

"Are you sure?" I asked.

"Yes," Kurkura replied. "I am positive. He has said, 'No.'"

# CHAPTER 25

# Are You Resting?

*The world is not to be put in order, the world is in order. It is for us to put ourselves in unison with this order.* —*Henry Miller*

Despite all the experiences I've had in Africa and the lessons I've learned, I still struggle for balance and peace. Just recently, I found myself having yet another bad day. It didn't begin that way, but by mid-morning, things really started to go south. The first tinges of a headache appeared, and I attempted to drown them out with one more cup of steaming black coffee. I had made commitments that now seemed impossible to meet. Things I assumed had been brought to completion, issues and transactions I thought had been safely put to bed, now began to unwind. The day kept getting worse. Over the noon hour, I had a business lunch with someone I didn't really enjoy being with and I became increasingly distracted. Things just kept going downhill. New problems seemed to emerge out of thin air, and by mid-afternoon I was a gnarled-up mess.

My family at home was happy and secure; my fellow employees seemed to be doing just fine. Nothing had really changed, but I had succeeded at working myself into an unexplainable, inextricable frenzy. I poured myself another cup of coffee. Just then, the intercom buzzed and I was informed that I had a phone call. "Take a message," I snapped. "I think the call might be from Africa," was the response.

That gave me considerable pause, and I somewhat reluctantly picked up the phone. It was my friend, Tekle Selassie, calling from Ethiopia. As you may know, there is typically a one- or two-second gap between transmission and reception on calls to and from Africa.

"Hi, Ward," came the high, accent-rich voice from my friend in Africa.

As I began to respond, I thought I heard the words, "Are you resting?"

"Sorry, Tekle. I missed that, but what I thought I heard you say was, 'Are you resting.'"

"Yes," came the simple reply.

"Tekle, my friend, I am so far from resting that you wouldn't be able to comprehend it. No, I'm not resting, absolutely not!"

"That's not what I meant," replied Tekle. "I meant, are you resting in the Lord?"

That gave me pause and it took me a moment or two to reply with a bit of chagrin, "No, Tekle, I need to be honest. I'm not resting in the Lord. I'm not resting at all."

His response still haunts and challenges me to this day: "If you're not resting in the Lord, how can you possibly be enjoying the Lord?"

Now I felt really bad—another swing and a miss in the life of Ward Brehm. In frustration, I responded, "Tekle, I haven't been enjoying the Lord, and I'm pretty sure He hasn't enjoyed me much either today."

After that, Tekle told me to take three deep breaths, and then he prayed for me in his uniquely Ethiopian way. Then we hung up.

That's it! I'm going home. I'm going to find a shady place, stretch out the hammock and rest in the Lord. I bailed out, and it actually felt pretty good!

A few days later, I was relating this experience to my mentor and confidant, Monty Sholund. He listened intently and patiently as I explained my newfound wisdom. When I finally finished, he said, "I don't think that's what Tekle meant." He went on to tell me a wonderful story. When he was a young boy, Monty traveled to the Hoover Dam. Standing in front of this incredible testament to mankind's ingenuity, he gazed at the turbine engines nearly ten stories tall. He asked the tour guide, "When do you turn them on?" "They're always on," came the response. "That's impossible! I can't hear a thing," said Monty. "That's because they are operating at perfect rest," came the answer.

These unimaginably huge engines and all of their working parts were whirling and spinning at extraordinary speeds fully in sync with one other, perfectly lubricated, in total alignment, with no foreign particles to disrupt. The machines were operating at perfect rest, under pressure, and generating tremendous pressure.

I was getting the point.

Monty further explained that nothing worthwhile can exist without pressure. A sailboat is stranded without the pressure of the wind; its beauty and grace lie in its ability to harness that pressure to propel it forward. A priceless Stradivarius violin creates true beauty only with the pressure of the bow; only constant pressure can create a masterpiece concerto.

It was starting to make more sense.

I'm pretty much a doer, not a whiner, so I picked up the pieces of that broken day and recommitted myself to being the most pressure-filled follower God ever had. Up to that point, I couldn't do enough. I wrote a book, organized trips to Africa, gave talks, led prayer discussion groups, tended to friends in the hospital, constantly communicated with Christian friends in Africa, and soon once again had my cup, if not overflowing, certainly filled to the brim. I recalled that God never promised to deliver us *from difficulty*, He only promised to deliver us *in difficulties.*

Then I was reading the book, *The 24-Hour Society, Understanding Human Limits In A World That Never Stops.* In it, Harvard sleep researcher Dr. Martin Moore describes the cycle of human consciousness. He explains that our needs for longer periods of sleep and rest are unusual in the animal kingdom. Most animals catnap, take their sleep and activity in smaller doses, and sustain any particular activity for shorter periods of time. But not human beings. We need longer periods of rest. A friend, Jim Brown from London, recalled a conversation with his grandfather, who was born in the late 1800s. His grandfather told him, "You need to rest the horses." When Jim asked what he meant, the grandfather said that when he was young, machinery did not exist that could run without rest. Animals were the main source of assistance in human endeavors, and they needed rest. This rest for the animals often led to a "forced rest" for humans. But now with cars, tractors, and machines, there was no longer a need for rest. He looked at Jim and said once again, "I would advise your generation to rest the horses."

For me, all the pieces began to fall into place. It isn't a matter of action or inaction, cause and effect, but the idea of letting God and His will be central to everything we do. It's being one with God and at perfect rest. That's much harder to *do* than to write about.

# CHAPTER 26

# Getting Back to Square One

*Blessedness lieth not in much and many, but in One and oneness.*
*—Theologica Germanica*

In past travels to Africa with groups of businessmen, we've come to label our day-to-day business lives as the "Cyclotron." It's as though we wake up in the morning, put on our "FBI suits" with starched collars and fashionable ties, and climb right into the belly of this dormant beast we call the Cyclotron. The anxieties and pressures of past days and events typically engage the ominous levers and gyroscopes. And we love it! At least at first. Each day is about new challenges, new goals, new heights, and new accomplishments. The adrenaline flows and the brain is engaged. And in the language of our prehistoric forefathers, "The hunt begins." Only, our missions are nowhere near as defined as they were in the past. They often have no clear beginning and, more often, no specific end. But with a sense of eager anticipation, or fear of failure, or dutiful obligation, we climb into the Cyclotron and fasten our seatbelts. The potential danger lies not in the effort or even the purpose, but rather in the process. We are so enticed by the action, so engaged in the sequence, that we lose ourselves in it.

Many of the Africans I have come in contact with over the past years have chided my Type A behavior, including my compulsion for organization and structure. They remind me that God created us as human "beings," not human "doings." Nevertheless, in Western society, so much of the value we place on our lives is based on what we do. During my first trip to Africa, I was confounded by the ever-posed request, "Tell us about yourself." I began by explaining that I owned a business in Minneapolis. They politely replied that they weren't interested in what I did for a living. They just wanted to know who I was. I told them about my interests, my hobbies, my love of travel, et cetera. They again gently reminded me that while this was somewhat interesting, they really wanted to know who I was. When I discussed my family, I could see that I was getting closer to what they wanted, but I would always walk away with the haunting question of whether I really knew who I was.

In many ways, Africa helped me discover myself. When I journeyed into the unknown with only faith for fuel, unwritten pages in my life were opened wide for the awesome, challenging, exhilarating, and always unexpected lessons and adventures that Africa gave. I experienced an enormous paradigm shift, not unlike those caused by catastrophic and heartbreaking personal occurrences. My life was turned upside down, though remarkably I'm sure I'm still standing right side up. My newfound faith and hope in God gave me different priorities and a new sense of direction. I now know that I am not alone. The strength of this conviction allows me to seek balance and meaning, fail, and seek again. It also gives me power to control my personal Cyclotron.

My friend Greg Snell is fond of saying, "Make sure you keep the main thing the main thing. He's referring to God's number one commandment: "Love your God with all your soul, and with all your might." It seems obvious that in order to love God, you need to know God. Yet I have found that it's often much easier to attempt to do things for God than to simply love Him and find rest in Him. I'm often guilty of running ahead of Him, and becoming so focused on deeds that I am too exhausted to spend quiet time with Him. All the while I know I desperately need more of Him.

These words of Eugene Peterson express the idea better than I ever could:

*I want to simplify your lives. When others are telling you to read more, I want to tell you to read less; when others are telling you to do more, I want to tell you to do less. The world does not need more of you; you need more of God. Your friends do not need more of you; you need more of God. For we do not progress in the Christian life by becoming more competent, more knowledgeable, more virtuous, or more energetic. We do not advance in the Christian life by acquiring expertise. Each day, and many times each day, we need more of God. 'Back to Square One,' God said.*

For me, getting back to Square One is the most challenging aspect of my faith journey. I like to do things and I can get things done. I like checklists and I like scorecards. I like contests and I enjoy races. And all of this can be a mighty distraction from God's call to humbly seek Him in a spirit of faithfulness and obedience. I always thought that what God really wanted was effectiveness. Now I think what He really wants is me.

CHAPTER 27

# Where Is Your Africa?

*"Freedom is useless if we don't exercise it as characters making choices..." We are free to change those stories by which we live because we are genuine characters and not mere puppets. We can choose our defining stories. We can do so because we actively participate in the creation of our stories. We are co-authors as well as characters. Few things are as encouraging as the realization that things can be different, and we have a role in making them so."*

—Daniel Taylor

*God did not call you to be canary-birds in a little cage, and to hop up and down on three sticks, within a space no larger than the size of a cage. God calls you to be eagles, and to fly from sun to sun, over continents.*          —Henry Ward Beecher

Many people believe that on September 11, 2001, our world dramatically changed. I'm not so sure that the world changed as much as our perspective on it. In the aftermath of the terrorist attack on America, the covers of our national magazines screamed out, "Why Do They Hate Us?" Prior to September 11, that question was seldom raised or discussed because we felt no threat and knew no better. Now Americas are trying to understand: "Who exactly are *they*?" It is clear that we have been mostly oblivious to the world outside our borders.

My own 9/11 wake-up call came in 1993 on my first trip to Africa. The foundations of most everything I had held to be true were shaken by my encounters with cultures and lifestyles far different than my own. Out of necessity, the world became my classroom.

The world isn't changing so much as it is shrinking. Borders that were months away are now only hours away. Cultures seemingly centuries apart are now melded together through travel, media, and communications. Events occurring in faraway places are instantly transcribed into our consciences through cable news. We see bombs dropping and communities torn apart. We see starving people, not just from a socio-economic perspective, but live on the nightly news. The world knows we are watching, and our response (or lack thereof) in large part is also communicated.

For many Americans, the United States is not only the center of the world, but it also *is* their world. Many would flunk even a basic world geography test. One-third of the members of the U.S. Congress do not have passports. A friend in a prominent role in our federal government recently referred to the ambassador of an African nation as being "Afro-American."

We think English is *the* world language. I was delighted by the response of a mother, who while shopping with her 10-year old son was able to teach a very valuable lesson. They were standing behind another mother and son, who both had heavy Eastern European accents, which were apparent from their conversation with the clerk. "Why does that boy talk so funny?" the American woman's son asked. "Well, all I know," his mother replied, "is that little boy speaks at least one more language than you do."

America is the wealthiest nation on earth. I believe many developing countries find it difficult to understand how we can have knowledge of starvation and death by curable infectious diseases, and not step in to alleviate these human tragedies. They find it difficult to understand how we can be comfortable and complacent in our world of material security, while they in turn struggle mightily just to survive each day.

I don't think most people in developing countries hate Americans, but the collision of cultures is fertile soil for alienation. The gap between prosperity and poverty is certainly widening. But I have found that the dreams and prayers of all people are always the same: safety and security; freedom and a better life for our children; a world in harmony; common ground; a foundation for bridges.

It's a long whistle and a few light years from the impossibly remote communities I visited on my long walk. For my friends I met along the riverbed in West Pokot, September 11th was a non-event. The Millennium was irrelevant. The war with Iraq and the massive military buildup in the Middle East are not factors in their lives. They live isolated and insulated in a much-less-than-perfect Shangri La on the far side of the mountain. They have learned how to survive despite seemingly insurmountable hardships and, in the process, they have placed their emphasis on community, family, and faith.

Ever since I went on that first adventure to Africa, I have wondered about the hold this strange and alluring continent has on me. In retrospect, I realize that by going to Africa, I not only wanted to change my paradigm, I wanted to change my life. From the outside looking in, my life was already seemingly blessed beyond measure. But something was missing. What was missing was purpose. What was missing was God.

I have long resisted putting a label on it, but I have recently come to realize that Africa is a calling on my life, a calling from God. I have no other explanation for the immense hold it has on me. In the past, I had always thought of missions and faith-based deeds as things you did for others—fulfilling perhaps, but mostly dull, and certainly not exciting or fun!  Well, I couldn't have been more wrong. This "calling" has indeed been the most thrilling and exhilarating ride of my life. It has taken me to strange and faraway places of timeless beauty and grace, and one of the greatest blessings has been the countless, deep friendships I have made along the way.

Personally, I needed to go to Africa to find God. I needed to get nine time zones away from computers, cell phones, e-mail, voicemails, faxes, and Palm Pilots. I needed to find a place where schedules and priorities and circumstances of home are quickly overwhelmed by the highly tangible life and death struggles taken up each day by people who nevertheless possess a rich and deep understanding of themselves, their communities, and God. For me, Africa became a cornerstone of meaning and represented an oasis of passion in an over-familiar life. It created the space for God.

Is a trip to Africa a prerequisite for finding God? Certainly not. But I do believe that every person needs to search to find his or her own "Africa." Poverty in many forms pollutes nearly every aspect of society across the entire planet. I believe God

wants us to discover those places, both faraway and next to home, where He is moving mountains, and to join Him there. Typically, we do just the opposite.

I have heard stories similar to mine of peoples' lives being changed: from orphanages in Russia to inner-city schools in Minneapolis, from the slums of Calcutta to remote medical clinics in the mountains of Afghanistan, from the streets of Washington, D.C., to the wretched prisons in Asia. Indeed, all across the world, people are answering the Biblical question,

"Who is my Neighbor?" And these people are finding themselves radically changed, engaged, and discovering meaning and relevance by being involved in things much bigger than themselves.

I believe that, deep down, most people would love to have God change their lives. Here's the thing: If asked, He will, every time, guaranteed. And while these changes may initially seem scary, they ultimately lay a foundation for a life filled with purpose and meaning.

Discovery, acceptance, and purpose have made this latest chapter in my life my most important. I have learned far more than I have taught. I have been helped much more than I have helped. I have received so much more than I have given.

I will be forever indebted to Africa. Africa awakened me when I didn't even know I was asleep. Africa allowed God to give me my own personal passageway to meaning and purpose. I pray that everyone who seeks one will find a similar path. I pray that each of you will find your own Africa.

# Acknowledgments

Writing this book has been a labor of love, which would have never been possible without the encouragement, support, and prayers I have received from so many.

First, my partner throughout this entire endeavor has been Evelyn Vida, whose gifts at editing and tremendous enthusiasm are hugely responsible for this work. Also, thanks to Jim Klobuchar, Michael Kimpur, Bob Seiple, Larry Julian, and Steve Moore for editorial comments on the manuscript.

Thanks to Arthur Rouner for initially inviting me to visit Africa, which ignited in me a great passion and calling to these faraway places.

I am forever indebted to Monty Sholund for mentoring, encouragement, and also prodding to get this manuscript down off the shelf many times.

I want to thank my assistant and friend Harriet Waltz, who entered every keystroke of the countless drafts and redrafts.

I want to thank my core group of friends here in Minnesota: Dave Durenberger, Mike Sime, and Steve Moore, as well as the "Boys of Tuesday," who meet each week to share our lives.

Thanks to all the praying friends in Washington, D.C., including Eric Fellman, Doug Coe, Bob Hunter, Kent Hotaling, Gary Haugen, Mark Powers, Glenn Powell, and Senators Jim Inhofe and Rod Grams. They all have left footprints on these experiences.

I thank the many, many friends in Africa who have been such a huge part of my journeys there: Greg and Deb Snell, Sam and Lynn Owen, Tekle Selassie, Abraham Fiseha, Gad Gasatura,

Prosper Turimuci, Bernard Barandereka, Charles Murigande, Agnes Mukabaranga, Garth Collins, Gary Tullis, Paulo and Sarah Kyama, Sam Poghisio, the late Samuel Nimubona, Kurkura Wafo, President and Anna Mkapa, Tim Kreutter, Lazaro Nyalandu, the staff of World Vision, and so many, many others.

To all the Windpump Teams, and especially Jeff Bird, Rich Cammack, Heidi Morgan, Jay Bennett, "Pokot" George Fulton, Bob Naegele, Bill Bieber, Dean Riesen, Mike Wikman, Tim Gagner, Denny Babcock, and Rich Voebel.

An obvious but special thanks to my family: my loving, praying, and supporting wife, Kris; and three of the greatest gifts I have received from God: sons Andy and Michael and daughter Sarah.

And, of course, my walking companion, John Lodinyo who, along with Philip, Mark, and James, in the simplicity of West Pokot taught me to ponder the complexities within my own soul.

Finally, the greatest thanks of all goes to God, who planted in my heart not only a deep passion for the people and places of Africa, but also the solid conviction that His hand continues to move in powerful ways across the faraway and too often forgotten continent of Africa.

**Also by Ward Brehm:**
**"Life Through A Different Lens"**

**All the author's royalties from these books
will support ongoing work in Africa**